a simple table

MICHELE CRANSTON

a simple table

Fresh and fabulous recipes for every day

with photography by
PETRINA TINSLAY

MURDOCH BOOKS

Contents

A simple table

This book started its life as a title or, to be more precise, an image of a plain white table with a bowl of beautiful food—food that was simple and pared back but still bursting with colour and flavour.

Once I had this image and the title of the book in my head, I started thinking about favourite foods. These foods weren't necessarily comforting in style, like a soup or Mum's favourite stew, but comforting in the sense that these are the flavours we all return to time and time again in the kitchen—things such as caramelised onions, freshly chopped parsley, tomatoes and olives or that just-squeezed lemon or lime.

I asked myself what makes a certain recipe a family favourite and why do some of the old classics just keep working for every generation? All of us, no matter how accomplished we are in the kitchen, will often find ourselves on a Wednesday night enjoying the same dish that we quite possibly had the previous week, like a roast chicken, a tuna pasta or a herby cheese omelette. They are our culinary default settings that we keep returning to because we know them, we like them and we feel comfortable with them. These are the kind of recipes I wanted in this book.

This isn't a book about clever food—there's no culinary gymnastics to delight a restaurant patron, there's no sous vide or liquid nitrogen party tricks and no mention of the word 'diet'—it's about food to come home to or share with family and friends. It's also a book that is, in many ways, a response to the various conversations that I've had in the schoolyard over the years, while waiting with the other parents for the home-time bell to ring. It's the answer to all those questions: 'What should I make for dinner?', 'What should I cook for friends on the weekend?', 'What's easy?' and 'How do you cook quinoa?'.

And so, the book formed itself into chapters of recipes that were all about how we eat and who we are eating with—food for gatherings, food for families and comfort food for lazy nights in front of the TV.

Two bowls is a chapter about the meals you make when you are home alone or just cooking for two. It's also the chapter for parents who want something a little more interesting for dinner while the kids are happy with a quick-fix pizza or pasta.

Four plates is all about family food, whether it's shared plates of corn fritters, schnitzels or baked snapper, or simple midweek roasts that will keep everyone happy.

One pot celebrates the idea of cooking everything together in one simple dish, and features warming, comfort food like meaty stews and flavoursome curries.

Weekend platters are the meals we cook for family and friends on weekends when there is more time to cook and more people gathered around the table.

On the side is a collection of favourite side dishes, which can be served as part of a weekend feast or to accompany a simple midweek barbecue, or to accompany many of the main meals in this book.

Pretty spoons is a chapter of simple, creamy desserts that combine indulgence and flirty fruitiness in one slightly sinful spoonful.

And lastly,

Teacups and cake plates is a chapter devoted to the simple joy of afternoon tea and home-baked cakes.

Whether we are enjoying a quick bowl of pasta with a friend or sharing a large weekend roast with the family, the very act of eating is a communal experience that is accompanied by the rattle of pots and pans, the clatter of plates and the jangle of cutlery, and it's that simple, everyday experience that this book celebrates. And so I hope that a few more family favourites will be added to your cooking repertoire and that this book will become a dog-eared companion to those family meals and occasional celebratory feasts that punctuate our daily lives.

two bowls

Pan-fried whiting with pomegranate salad

Everyone seems to have a preferred method of removing the arils, or fleshy red seeds, from pomegranates, but I think this method is the easiest and most fun. Slice the pomegranate in half and place both halves in a large snaplock bag. Give the pomegranate halves a squeeze to loosen the arils, then seal the bag. Using a wooden spoon, give the rounded skin of the pomegranate several firm smacks—this should dislodge the arils. If not, give the rounds a firmer squeeze and then repeat the process. Pour the juice and arils into a bowl and remove any of the white pith.

35 g (1¹/₄ oz/¹/₄ cup) plain (all-purpose) flour
50 g (1³/₄ oz/¹/₄ cup) instant polenta
¹/₂ teaspoon sumac
¹/₄ teaspoon ground white pepper
300 g (10¹/₂ oz) whiting fillets
2 zucchini (courgettes), finely diced
2 Lebanese (short) cucumbers, finely diced
1 celery stalk, diced
20 g (³/₄ oz/1 cup) flat-leaf (Italian) parsley leaves
90 g (3¹/₄ oz/¹/₂ cup) pomegranate arils
1 tablespoon extra virgin olive oil
60 g (2¹/₄ oz) butter
lemon wedges, to serve

Put the flour in a large snaplock bag with the polenta, sumac and white pepper and season with sea salt. Seal and shake to combine. Open the bag and add the whiting fillets. Seal the bag again and shake gently to coat the fish in the seasoned flour.

Put the zucchini, cucumber, celery, parsley and pomegranate arils in a bowl. Season with sea salt and freshly ground black pepper and drizzle with the olive oil.

Heat the butter in a large frying pan over medium heat and fry the whiting fillets for 2–3 minutes on each side, or until golden and the thickest part of the fillet is cooked through.

Divide the zucchini and pomegranate salad between two pasta bowls and top with the fried whiting. Serve with the lemon wedges.

SERVES 2

The pomegranate brings a lovely tartness to this salad, and balances the richness of the fried fish.

Poached chicken and mango salad

The onion adds a lovely richness and texture to this dish, so make sure you are patient and cook it to the sweet, almost-burnt caramel stage. If you do, the flavour will work beautifully with the mango and lime.

This is a great salad if you're looking for something to make with left-over roast chicken; otherwise, poach a chicken breast fillet using the method on page 20.

60 ml (2 fl oz/¼ cup) extra virgin olive oil
1 red chilli, seeded and finely chopped
1 red onion, thinly sliced
1 tablespoon tamarind purée
2 teaspoons grated palm sugar (jaggery) or light brown sugar
1 teaspoon soy sauce
1 tablespoon lime juice
175 g (6 oz/1 cup) shredded cooked chicken
1 mango, flesh cut into thin wedges
½ Lebanese (short) cucumber, diced
8 mint leaves, thinly sliced
1 handful coriander (cilantro) leaves
100 g (3½ oz) baby salad leaves
1 tablespoon toasted sesame seeds

Put the olive oil, chilli and onion in a frying pan over medium heat and cook for 10 minutes, stirring occasionally, or until the onion is quite caramelised and almost burnt.

Meanwhile, put the tamarind purée and 60 ml (2 fl oz/¼ cup) water in a large bowl. Add the palm sugar, soy sauce and lime juice and stir until the sugar has dissolved. Add the chicken, mango, cucumber, mint and half of the coriander leaves. Toss gently to combine.

Divide the salad leaves between two large bowls and arrange the chicken and mango salad over the top. Garnish with the caramelised onion, the remaining coriander leaves and a sprinkle of sesame seeds.

SERVES 2

Prawn salad with pearl couscous

A zesty Asian-style salad that just screams 'summer', this recipe can of course be enjoyed at any time of the year, whenever you feel like the refreshing flavours of lime, cucumber and fresh herbs. If you prefer, replace the prawns with chargrilled squid or poached chicken.

I've used pearl couscous here—a large, round couscous—because of its slightly chewy texture and its ability to soak up the lovely flavours of the dressing. It's sometimes called Israeli couscous or moghrabieh; look for it in delis or Middle Eastern supermarkets.

40 g (1½ oz/¼ cup) pearl couscous
125 ml (4 fl oz/½ cup) boiling water
2 tablespoons caster (superfine) sugar
1 tablespoon lime juice
1½ tablespoons fish sauce
1 tablespoon rice vinegar
12 large (500 g/1 lb 2 oz) cooked prawns (shrimp), peeled and deveined, tails left intact
2 vine-ripened tomatoes, finely diced
1 long red chilli, seeded and finely chopped
2 kaffir lime leaves, thinly sliced
1 Lebanese (short) cucumber, finely diced
1 handful mint leaves
1 handful coriander (cilantro) leaves
1 handful Thai basil leaves

Put the pearl couscous in a small saucepan and pour in the boiling water. Cover the pan and simmer over low heat for 5 minutes, or until all the water has been absorbed. Remove from the heat and drain.

Put the sugar, lime juice, fish sauce and vinegar in a bowl and stir until the sugar has dissolved. Add the prawns, tomato, chilli, lime leaves and couscous. Toss to combine, then set aside for a few minutes to allow the prawns and couscous to absorb some of the flavours.

Add the cucumber and fresh mint, coriander and Thai basil. Toss once more before dividing between two bowls.

SERVES 2

Green pea salad with ricotta and prosciutto

This salad is all about the play between the milky richness of the ricotta, the minty freshness of the peas and the salty sweetness of the prosciutto, so please only use the best ingredients —and by that I mean freshly sliced prosciutto and a thick wedge of full-fat ricotta from the delicatessen. Don't use the supermarket ricotta that comes in a tub, which I'll admit does have its culinary uses, but not in this salad.

140 g (5 oz/1 cup) frozen peas
100 g (3½ oz) sugar snap peas, trimmed
10 mint leaves, thinly sliced
2 teaspoons red wine vinegar
2 tablespoons extra virgin olive oil
1 small head of radicchio, cut into thin wedges
6 slices prosciutto, halved
115 g (4 oz/½ cup) fresh full-fat ricotta cheese
1 tablespoon pine nuts, toasted

Bring a large saucepan of salted water to the boil. Add the peas and cook for 3 minutes, then add the sugar snap peas and cook for a further 3 minutes.

Meanwhile, put the mint, vinegar and olive oil in a bowl and season with sea salt and freshly ground black pepper. Drain the cooked peas and put them in the bowl with the mint and dressing. Stir to coat the peas.

Arrange the radicchio wedges in the base of two large shallow bowls. Top with the prosciutto, ricotta and dressed peas, then sprinkle with the pine nuts.

SERVES 2

Fresh tomato and olive tortiglioni

I'm often asked about kitchen essentials and meals for the time-poor, and this recipe answers both queries. I always have pasta and extra virgin olive oil in the cupboard; parmesan, olives, parsley and bacon in the fridge; and a bowl of lemons and ripening tomatoes on the kitchen bench. With these simple ingredients on hand, you can whip up a delicious meal in minutes.

4 vine-ripened tomatoes, coarsely chopped
1 teaspoon sea salt
10 pitted kalamata olives, coarsely chopped
15 basil leaves, thinly sliced
1 handful flat-leaf (Italian) parsley leaves, coarsely chopped
200 g (7 oz) tortiglioni or penne pasta
35 g (1^{1}/4 oz/^{1}/3 cup) finely grated parmesan cheese
60 ml (2 fl oz/^{1}/4 cup) extra virgin olive oil

Put the chopped tomatoes in a bowl along with the sea salt, olives, basil and parsley. Stir gently to ensure all the tomato pieces are well seasoned, then set aside.

Bring a large saucepan of salted water to the boil and add the pasta. Cook until *al dente*, then drain the pasta and return to the warm pan.

Add the parmesan and olive oil to the pasta and stir to combine, then add the tomato mixture. Season with freshly ground black pepper, toss together and then divide between two warmed pasta bowls.

SERVES 2

This fresh tomato pasta is best made in summer when the tomatoes are ruby red and full of flavour.

Lemongrass-poached chicken with harissa tomatoes

If you like, you can poach the chicken for this recipe the day before—simply follow the method given here, reserving some of the poaching liquid. Then, when the chicken is cool, shred the meat and put it into a container before pouring over some of the reserved poaching liquid, adding a little more seasoning or freshly chopped herbs for extra flavour. This is a great method for cooking chicken for any salad or sandwich, and will ensure the meat retains its juiciness.

LEMONGRASS-POACHED CHICKEN
1 teaspoon sea salt
90 g (3¼ oz/1 bunch) coriander (cilantro), rinsed well
1 lemongrass stem, white part only, rinsed and coarsely chopped
4 cm (1½ inch) piece fresh ginger, peeled and sliced
1 lemon, juiced
2 boneless, skinless chicken breast fillets

1 tablespoon olive oil
1 teaspoon ground cumin
1 teaspoon ground coriander
2 garlic cloves, finely chopped
1 red onion, thinly sliced
3 ripe roma (plum) tomatoes, cut into wedges
1 tablespoon harissa
lime wedges, to serve

To poach the chicken, fill a large saucepan with 1 litre (35 fl oz/4 cups) water and add the sea salt. Remove the stems and roots from the coriander and add to the water, reserving the leaves for later. Add the lemongrass, ginger and 1 tablespoon of the lemon juice to the water and bring to the boil. When the water has reached a slow boil, add the chicken breasts and return to the boil, then cover with a lid and remove the pan from the heat. Set aside for 20 minutes to allow the residual heat to gently poach the chicken.

Heat the olive oil in a non-stick frying pan over medium heat and add the cumin, coriander, garlic and onion. Cook, stirring occasionally, for 3 minutes, or until the onion is soft and the spices are fragrant. Add the tomatoes and harissa and cook for about 2 minutes, or until the tomatoes are soft. Add the remaining lemon juice and a handful of roughly chopped coriander leaves.

Remove the chicken from the poaching liquid and thinly slice against the grain. Divide the chicken between two bowls, top with the cooked tomatoes and garnish with the remaining coriander. Serve with the lime wedges and a simple cucumber salad or steamed couscous.

SERVES 2

Quinoa salad with tuna and preserved lemon

Quinoa is a South American grain that is high in protein and very nourishing, as it contains all eight essential amino acids. Although quinoa comes in many varieties, the most common are white, red and black, or a mixture of the three. My preference is the mix, but you can use whatever is available. If you haven't yet fallen under the quinoa spell, then use steamed rice, couscous or risoni pasta instead.

100 g (3½ oz/½ cup) tri-coloured quinoa
100 g (3½ oz) green beans, trimmed and halved lengthways
2 tablespoons lemon juice
2 tablespoons extra virgin olive oil
1 tablespoon finely chopped preserved lemon rind
20 g (¾ oz/1 bunch) chives, snipped
40 g (1½ oz) baby salad leaves
250 g (9 oz/1 punnet) cherry tomatoes, halved
200 g (7 oz) tinned tuna in oil, drained and flaked

Put the quinoa in a saucepan with 250 ml (9 fl oz/1 cup) water and bring to the boil. Cover the pan, then reduce the heat to low and simmer for 10 minutes. Remove the pan from the heat and set aside, with the lid still on, and allow the grains to gently steam for 4–5 minutes.

Bring another saucepan of salted water to the boil and blanch the green beans for about 2 minutes, or until they are emerald green. Drain and rinse under cold running water.

Meanwhile, to make a dressing, combine the lemon juice, olive oil, preserved lemon and chives in a large bowl. Add the quinoa to the bowl and stir to coat in the dressing.

Divide the salad leaves between two bowls. Top with the tomatoes and beans, then spoon over the quinoa. Top with the tuna and serve.

SERVES 2

When using preserved lemon, remove the pithy flesh and only use the rind. Don't throw the salty flesh away: keep it in the jar and use it as a flavouring on roast lamb or chicken.

Broccolini and anchovy pasta

I'm a bit of a fan of broccolini, as I prefer its softer texture, especially in a pasta recipe like this, but this will work just as well with broccoli—just cut it into small florets. What makes this pasta dish really sing, however, is the anchovies, so if you're not keen on them, you probably should turn the page.

200 g (7 oz) casarecce pasta
60 ml (2 fl oz/1/4 cup) olive oil
20 g (3/4 oz) butter
2 garlic cloves, finely chopped
6 anchovies, finely chopped
2 long red chillies, seeded and finely chopped
300 g (10 1/2 oz/2 bunches) broccolini, sliced into 3 cm (1 1/4 inch) lengths
1 tablespoon lemon juice
25 g (1 oz/1/4 cup) finely grated parmesan cheese

Bring a large saucepan of salted water to the boil and add the pasta. Cook until *al dente*, then drain well.

Meanwhile, heat the olive oil in a large non-stick frying pan over medium heat. Add the butter, garlic, anchovies and chilli and stir for 2 minutes, then add the broccolini and lemon juice and cook for a further 5 minutes, or until the broccolini is tender.

Transfer the pasta to the frying pan, add half of the parmesan and stir to combine well. Spoon into two warmed pasta bowls and sprinkle over the remaining parmesan.

SERVES 2

Spinach carbonara

A classic dish that manages to combine both refined elegance and home-style comfort in one delicious mouthful, spinach carbonara is a must for everyone's repertoire as it can be pulled together in minutes and makes for a perfect late-night supper, a warming lunch or midweek meal. I've added spinach leaves to make it a bit healthier, but feel free to add the spinach to a green side salad instead.

200 g (7 oz) orecchiette pasta
1 tablespoon extra virgin olive oil
10 g (1/4 oz) butter
100 g (3 1/2 oz) rindless bacon rashers, thinly sliced
60 ml (2 fl oz/1/4 cup) white wine
2 large free-range eggs
35 g (1 1/4 oz/1/3 cup) finely grated parmesan cheese
125 g (4 1/2 oz/2 1/2 cups) baby English spinach leaves
2 tablespoons chopped flat-leaf (Italian) parsley

Bring a large saucepan of salted water to the boil and add the pasta. Cook until *al dente*, then drain well.

Meanwhile, put the olive oil and butter in a large, deep-sided non-stick frying pan. Add the bacon and fry over medium heat for about 2 minutes, or until the bacon is golden and crispy. Remove and drain on paper towel. Add the wine to the pan and cook for 1 minute to deglaze.

Put the eggs and half of the parmesan in a bowl and whisk to combine. Season with sea salt and freshly ground black pepper.

Transfer the pasta to the frying pan and toss over low heat to warm through, then add the spinach and whisked eggs. When the sauce has begun to thicken and coat the pasta, remove from the heat and divide between two warmed pasta bowls. Top with the bacon, the remaining parmesan and the parsley.

SERVES 2

Soba noodle salad with hot-smoked salmon

Years ago I worked in a café where we made this dressing using cup measures rather than tablespoons. The dressing was ladled out of a large preserving jar and drizzled over a tuna salad. The ginger–sesame flavours in the dressing are delicious, and if you love noodle salads and make them often, then I recommend you make a large batch of the dressing and store it in a glass jar in the fridge. It only improves with age and is beautiful drizzled over noodles, salads, chicken and seafood.

To make fast work of the vegetable preparation, use a mandolin to julienne the daikon and cucumber.

GINGER–SESAME DRESSING
1^1/2 tablespoons soy sauce
1^1/2 tablespoons sesame oil
2 teaspoons balsamic vinegar
2 tablespoons lime juice
1 tablespoon caster (superfine) sugar
1 tablespoon finely grated fresh ginger
1 tablespoon finely chopped lemongrass, white part only

150 g (5^1/2 oz) dried soba (buckwheat) noodles
150 g (5^1/2 oz) daikon (white radish), peeled and julienned
1 Lebanese (short) cucumber, julienned
8 snow peas (mangetout), trimmed and thinly sliced
^{1}/2 red capsicum (pepper), thinly sliced
1 handful coriander (cilantro) leaves
250 g (9 oz) hot-smoked salmon fillet, halved
lime wedges, to serve

To make the ginger–sesame dressing, put all the ingredients in a large bowl and stir to combine well.

Bring a large saucepan of salted water to the boil and add the soba noodles. Stir so the noodles don't stick together. When the water returns to the boil, add 125 ml (4 fl oz/^{1}/2 cup) of cold water and allow the water to return to the boil again. Repeat this process twice more, then drain the noodles and put them in the bowl with the dressing. Toss to coat the noodles.

Divide the noodles between two large pasta bowls and top with the julienned and sliced vegetables, coriander and a piece of salmon. Drizzle with any remaining dressing. Serve with the lime wedges.

SERVES 2

Avocado, bacon and watercress salad

This is one of those salads that's all about a balance of flavours. The horseradish and watercress deliver a hot, peppery bite, which is, in turn, softened by the richness of the avocado and bacon and the light freshness of the celery and tomato.

HORSERADISH DRESSING
1 tablespoon horseradish cream
1 tablespoon extra virgin olive oil
2 teaspoons lemon juice
1/2 teaspoon light brown sugar

4 rindless bacon rashers, roughly chopped
1 red onion, thinly sliced
60 g (2¼ oz/2 cups) watercress sprigs
2 ripe avocados
1 large roma (plum) tomato, diced
2 celery stalks, thinly sliced

To make the horseradish dressing, combine the horseradish cream, olive oil, lemon juice and brown sugar in a bowl. Stir to combine, then season with freshly ground black pepper.

Heat a non-stick frying pan over medium heat and add the bacon. Cook until browned and crispy, then remove with a slotted spoon and drain on paper towel. Add the onion to the pan and cook for 5–8 minutes, or until soft.

Divide the watercress between two bowls. Cut the avocados in half and remove the stones. Using a large spoon, remove each avocado from its skin and then slice it in half again to make a thick wedge. Nestle the avocado quarters into the watercress. Top with the fried bacon and onion, the tomato and celery and drizzle with the horseradish dressing.

SERVES 2

Ricotta and cavolo nero gnocchi with sage butter

I'll be the first to admit that home-made gnocchi doesn't fall into the throw-it-all-in-a-bowl, quick-and-easy-recipe category, but it is fun to make, tastes delicious and really isn't as hard as you might think. Anyway, let's face it: making your own gnocchi is guaranteed to give you that smug-in-the-kitchen smile.

The warm sage butter is also perfect to spoon over a simple pasta of roast pumpkin, pine nuts and English spinach.

200 g (7 oz) cavolo nero or Tuscan cabbage, stalks removed
70 g (2½ oz) butter
1 onion, finely chopped
1 garlic clove, finely chopped
35 g (1¼ oz/¼ cup) plain (all-purpose) flour
115 g (4 oz/½ cup) fresh full-fat ricotta cheese
1 large free-range egg yolk
50 g (2 oz/½ cup) finely grated parmesan cheese
1 teaspoon finely grated lemon zest
⅛ teaspoon ground white pepper
10 small sage leaves
shaved parmesan cheese, to serve

Blanch the cavolo nero leaves in a large saucepan of boiling water for 1 minute, or until soft and wilted, then drain and rinse under cold water. Squeeze the leaves to remove the excess liquid and then pat dry with paper towel. Chop the leaves very, very finely (to make it easier to incorporate into the ricotta).

Heat 20 g (¾ oz) of the butter in a frying pan over low heat. Add the onion and garlic and cook for 8–10 minutes, or until soft but not coloured. Stir in the cavolo nero. Transfer the mixture to a large bowl, add the flour and ricotta and mix well. Stir in the egg yolk, grated parmesan and lemon zest and season with the white pepper and a little sea salt.

Using 2 tablespoons, shape the mixture into 16 quenelles or rounded gnocchi and place them on a lightly floured tray. Place the gnocchi in the refrigerator to chill for at least 1 hour.

Bring a large saucepan of salted water to the boil. Add half the gnocchi to the water and cook for about 3 minutes, or until the gnocchi rise to the surface of the water. Using a slotted spoon or a small sieve, scoop the gnocchi out of the water and put them into a warmed pasta bowl. Repeat the process with the remaining gnocchi.

Meanwhile, put the remaining 50 g (1¾ oz) of butter and the sage leaves in a small frying pan and cook over medium heat until the butter has melted and the sage leaves are crisp. Spoon the sage leaves and butter over the gnocchi and garnish with some shaved parmesan.

SERVES 2

Chickpea and salami salad

Tinned chickpeas are one of those great store cupboard essentials that make it really easy to throw together a quick meal, from the simplest salads to hearty soups. They can be blended to make a dip, stirred into a warming vegetable casserole or simply dressed in olive oil and Moroccan spices and served alongside any grilled meat. In this salad, the flavour of the spicy salami works its way into the sweet roast tomatoes, while the chickpeas add an earthy balance and take it from being a light salad to a more substantial meal.

2 large, ripe roma (plum) tomatoes
8 slices hot salami
3 celery stalks, thinly sliced
400 g (14 oz) tinned chickpeas, drained and rinsed
1 handful flat-leaf (Italian) parsley leaves
1 tablespoon balsamic vinegar
2 tablespoons extra virgin olive oil
50 g (1¾ oz) baby rocket (arugula) leaves
12 small black olives

Preheat the oven to 180°C (350°F). Line a baking tray with baking paper.

Cut each tomato into four thick slices and place on the prepared tray. Season with sea salt and freshly ground black pepper, then top each tomato with a slice of salami. Cook the tomatoes for 15 minutes, or until the salami starts to become crisp around the edges. Remove from the oven. Using a pair of kitchen scissors, cut each tomato and salami in half.

Put the celery, chickpeas and parsley in a bowl with the vinegar and olive oil. Toss to combine.

Divide the rocket between two large bowls and top with the dressed chickpeas, then the warm tomato and salami. Scatter some olives over the top of each salad.

SERVES 2

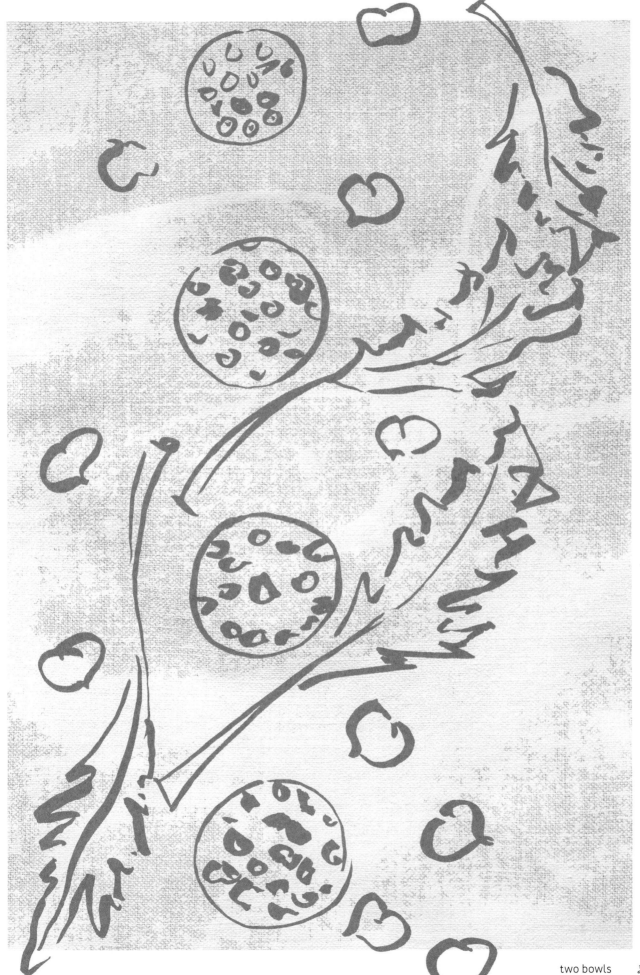

Smoked river trout salad with wild rice and watercress

I love watercress but I know lots of people think it's a bother to prepare. So, here's my tip for taming that wild bunch of greenery. Slice away the thick lower stems and untie the bunch. Place the watercress in a large bowl of water and rinse it well; this will also perk up the leaves. Leave it in the water for a few minutes while you line a plastic storage container with paper towel. Put on your favourite music and then set about removing the top sprigs and any nice leaves from the bunch. Think of it as a couple of minutes of quiet meditation! Put the picked leaves in the container, then cover and store in the fridge.

110 g (3³/₄ oz/¹/₂ cup) brown rice
50 g (1³/₄ oz/¹/₄ cup) wild rice
¹/₄ red onion, finely diced
1 tablespoon finely chopped preserved lemon rind
8 mint leaves, finely chopped
¹/₂ teaspoon ras el hanout
100 g (3¹/₂ oz) smoked river trout, flaked
2 handfuls watercress sprigs
2 soft-boiled free-range eggs
60 g (2¹/₄ oz) good-quality mayonnaise or lemon–mustard mayonnaise (page 166)

Put the brown rice and wild rice in a small saucepan and cover with 750 ml (26 fl oz/3 cups) of cold water. Bring to the boil, then reduce the heat to medium and cook for 30 minutes, or until the rice is tender.

Drain the rice and put it in a bowl with the onion, preserved lemon, mint, ras el hanout and flaked trout. Season with sea salt and freshly ground black pepper and toss to combine.

Divide the watercress between two large bowls. Spoon the rice and trout salad over the watercress. Peel the eggs and halve them, then arrange the eggs on the salad. Serve with a spoonful of mayonnaise.

SERVES 2

Once you've picked the watercress into sprigs, you'll be surprised how often you use it—scatter it over any salad or serve it alongside grilled fish or chicken.

Cheese and spinach frittata

This is a beautifully simple meal that is the perfect solution to a weekend brunch, a late-night supper or even a quick midweek lunch, when a slice of cheese and a cracker just won't do.

4 large free-range eggs
25 g (1 oz) butter
1 leek, white part only, rinsed and finely chopped
120 g (4¼ oz) English spinach leaves
115 g (4 oz/½ cup) fresh full-fat ricotta cheese
1 tablespoon finely chopped flat-leaf (Italian) parsley
2 tablespoons finely grated parmesan cheese

Put the eggs in a bowl and whisk to combine. Season with sea salt and freshly ground black pepper.

Heat the butter in a heavy-based frying pan over medium heat. Add the leek and cook, stirring occasionally, for about 5 minutes, or until the leek is golden and soft. Add the spinach leaves and cook until just wilted.

Pour the eggs over the spinach and leek, then add the ricotta in small scattered spoonfuls. Cook for 3–5 minutes, or until the egg is almost cooked through, then sprinkle the parsley and parmesan over the top.

Place the pan under a hot grill (broiler) to give the top a lovely golden finish and to ensure the frittata is cooked through.

Cut the frittata into wedges and serve in two warmed pasta bowls, with buttery wholemeal (whole-wheat) toast or warm crusty bread.

SERVES 2

Lemon pasta with garlic prawns

Midweek meals are often those dishes that we just throw together without too much thought, and this one has become one of my favourites. The flavours are fresh but the pasta makes it comforting, and although the ingredients are simple, the prawns make it feel a bit special. It's the perfect Wednesday night pick-me-up.

2 tablespoons lemon juice
200 g (7 oz) linguine
60 ml (2 fl oz/¼ cup) light olive oil
2 long red chillies, seeded and finely chopped
2 garlic cloves, finely chopped
12 raw king prawns (jumbo shrimp), peeled and deveined, tails left intact
250 g (9 oz/1 punnet) cherry tomatoes, halved
1 handful flat-leaf (Italian) parsley leaves
6 basil leaves
1 tablespoon snipped chives

Bring a large saucepan of salted water to the boil and add 1 tablespoon of the lemon juice, then add the linguine. Cook until *al dente*, then drain the pasta and return to the warm saucepan.

Meanwhile, heat the olive oil in a frying pan over medium heat. Add the chilli and garlic, stir to combine, then add the prawns. Cook the prawns for 3–4 minutes, turning once, until they are pink on both sides and beginning to curl. Add the tomatoes and cook for a further 1 minute. Remove from the heat.

Add the prawn mixture to the pasta along with the fresh herbs and the remaining 1 tablespoon of lemon juice. Season with sea salt and freshly ground black pepper and toss to combine. Divide the pasta and prawns between two warmed pasta bowls.

SERVES 2

Soy-simmered vegetables with tofu

Sometimes in winter you need a recipe that ticks both the healthy and comforting boxes. This bowl full of simmered vegetables is not only warming and invigorating, but tastes incredibly healthy. I think it has something to do with the soy and ginger broth, which to me always feels a bit medicinal, but in a good way.

If you can't find fresh shiitake mushrooms, use dried—they just need to be soaked in hot water for 10 minutes to soften them. Add the soaking liquid to the broth for an extra flavour kick.

300 g (10½ oz) silken tofu
2 tablespoons soy sauce
2 teaspoons sesame oil
125 ml (4 fl oz/½ cup) shaoxing rice wine
125 ml (4 fl oz/½ cup) mirin
2 star anise
1 garlic clove, thinly sliced
1 tablespoon finely grated fresh ginger
6 fresh shiitake mushrooms, halved
250 g (9 oz) daikon (white radish), peeled and sliced
250 g (9 oz) pumpkin (winter squash), peeled and cut into chunks
½ red capsicum (pepper), cut into 2 cm (¾ inch) squares
½ yellow capsicum (pepper), cut into 2 cm (¾ inch) squares
2 spring onions (scallions), cut into 2 cm (¾ inch) lengths
2 tablespoons Asian fried shallots

Drain the water from the tofu, then sit the tofu block on a few pieces of paper towel to absorb any extra liquid.

Meanwhile, put the soy sauce, sesame oil, rice wine, mirin, star anise, garlic and ginger in a large saucepan. Add the mushrooms, daikon and pumpkin, then pour in 125 ml (4 fl oz/½ cup) water. Bring to the boil over high heat, then reduce the heat to low and cook for 10 minutes. Add the red and yellow capsicum and the spring onion and cook for a further 5 minutes.

Cut the tofu into 2 cm (¾ inch) cubes and divide between two large bowls. Spoon the vegetables and broth over the top and garnish with the fried shallots.

SERVES 2

four plates

Lamb cutlets with zucchini and black quinoa salad

My son, rather expensively, loves a lamb cutlet. I think it has something to do with meat having a 'handle'. Surprisingly, he's not as excited by the zucchini and quinoa salad but that suits me fine—he gets the larger share of the cutlets and I get a larger serving of the salad.

Despite what he thinks, this is a delicious salad, which can be enjoyed with any grilled red meat. If serving the salad with beef, then swap the mint for basil.

12 lamb cutlets or lamb chops
1 tablespoon olive oil
$1/2$ teaspoon finely chopped rosemary
100 g ($31/2$ oz/$1/2$ cup) black quinoa
60 ml (2 fl oz/$1/4$ cup) extra virgin olive oil
2 long red chillies, seeded and thinly sliced
2 garlic cloves, crushed
400 g (14 oz) zucchini (courgettes), thickly sliced on the diagonal
1 tablespoon lemon juice
12 mint leaves, finely chopped
2 spring onions (scallions), thinly sliced
200 g (7 oz/1 punnet) yellow cherry tomatoes, halved

Place the lamb cutlets on a tray. Rub the olive oil over the cutlets and then sprinkle with the rosemary.

Put the quinoa in a saucepan with 250 ml (9 fl oz/1 cup) water and bring to the boil. Cover with the lid, then reduce the heat to low and simmer for 10 minutes. Remove the pan from the heat and set aside, with the lid still on, and allow the grains to gently steam for 4–5 minutes.

Meanwhile, heat the extra virgin olive oil in a non-stick frying pan over medium heat. Add the chilli and garlic and cook for 1 minute before adding the zucchini. Sauté for 8–10 minutes, or until the zucchini begins to soften and turns golden brown. Remove from the heat.

Transfer the cooked quinoa to a salad bowl and add the zucchini, lemon juice, mint, spring onion and tomatoes. Season generously with sea salt and freshly ground black pepper and stir to combine.

Preheat a barbecue grill or chargrill pan to medium–high. Cook the cutlets for 2–3 minutes on each side, or until cooked to your liking. Transfer to a warm serving plate and season with sea salt. Cover with foil and rest for a few minutes. Serve the lamb cutlets with the zucchini and quinoa salad.

SERVES 4

San choy bau

I've called this flavoursome bowl of minced pork san choy bau because of the way we've served it in this photo, which is one of my favourite ways to enjoy it in summer. However, the pork is just as delicious spooned over a bowl of noodles as an Asian twist on bolognese, or over some steamed rice for a perfectly comforting and wintery midweek meal.

2 tablespoons olive oil
4 spring onions (scallions), white part only, thinly sliced
4 garlic cloves, crushed
60 g (2¼ oz/¼ cup) finely grated fresh ginger
3 large red chillies, seeded and thinly sliced
500 g (1 lb 2 oz) minced (ground) pork
250 ml (9 fl oz/1 cup) white wine
2 tablespoons black bean and garlic sauce
2 tablespoons Chinese black vinegar
1 tablespoon light brown sugar
1 tablespoon sesame oil
100 g (3½ oz) fresh shiitake mushrooms, sliced
100 g (3½ oz) tinned water chestnuts, diced
iceberg lettuce cups, thinly sliced red capsicum (pepper), thinly sliced cucumber and mixed Asian herbs, to serve
chilli sauce, to serve

Heat the olive oil in a wok or deep-sided frying pan over high heat. Add the spring onion, garlic, ginger and chilli and stir-fry for 2 minutes, or until fragrant. Add the pork to the wok and stir-fry for 2–3 minutes, or until cooked through.

Add the wine and cook over high heat until reduced by half. Add the black bean sauce, vinegar, brown sugar, sesame oil and sliced mushrooms. Simmer, uncovered, stirring occasionally, for 8–10 minutes, or until the mixture has thickened and the mushrooms have completely softened. When ready to serve, stir through the water chestnuts.

Serve the pork with the lettuce cups, capsicum, cucumber and a handful of mixed Asian herbs. Serve with a side dish of chilli sauce.

SERVES 4

Chicken schnitzel with tabouleh salad

I think I've inherited my father's suspicion of buying things ready-coated in breadcrumbs, or maybe I just like the process of making it myself. Whatever the reason, I always make chicken schnitzel from scratch. It's one way to ensure the chicken is of the best quality, and the panko—parmesan crust is so deliciously crispy that you'll never return to soggy shop-bought schnitzel again. The parmesan adds a lovely richness to the crust that works well with the tabouleh salad but it's not essential, so if your children aren't fans of parmesan, then just drop it from the recipe.

2 boneless, skinless chicken breast fillets
35 g (1¼ oz/¼ cup) plain (all-purpose) flour
2 free-range eggs, lightly beaten
60 g (2¼ oz/1 cup) panko breadcrumbs
2 tablespoons finely grated parmesan cheese
60 ml (2 fl oz/¼ cup) vegetable oil
20 g (¾ oz) butter

TABOULEH
45 g (1½ oz/¼ cup) burghul (bulgur)
2 large ripe roma (plum) tomatoes, diced
120 g (4¼ oz/1 bunch) flat-leaf (Italian) parsley, finely chopped
10 mint leaves, finely chopped
¼ red onion, thinly sliced
60 ml (2 fl oz/¼ cup) extra virgin olive oil
1 tablespoon lemon juice

Cut each chicken breast in half lengthways. Place one of the chicken pieces between two sheets of baking paper and, using a meat mallet or rolling pin, pound the chicken to flatten it. Repeat with the remaining three pieces of chicken.

Put the flour, egg and breadcrumbs in three separate shallow bowls. Add the parmesan to the breadcrumbs and stir to combine.

Working with one piece of chicken at a time, dust the chicken with flour, dip into the egg and then press into the breadcrumbs. Set aside on a tray lined with baking paper.

To make the tabouleh, put the burghul in a small bowl and cover with boiling water. Set aside for 5 minutes, then drain the burghul and transfer to a large bowl. Add the remaining ingredients, season with sea salt and freshly ground black pepper and stir to combine.

Heat the oil and butter in a large non-stick frying pan over medium–high heat. When the butter has melted and is bubbling a little, fry the chicken pieces for 8–10 minutes, turning halfway through, or until dark golden on both sides. Drain on paper towel. Serve the chicken schnitzels with the tabouleh salad.

SERVES 4

Other serving suggestions:

~~ In summer, the richness of the schnitzel can be offset with a light, healthy salad. The tabouleh works well, but if you are looking for other options, here are a few.

~~ Make a springtime potato salad by tossing together warm boiled potato chunks with thinly sliced spring onions (scallions) and roughly chopped parsley, mint, dill and chives. Dress with a lemon vinaigrette.

~~ Make an Asian-style salad by combining thinly sliced snow peas (mangetout), red capsicum (pepper), cucumber and carrot with bean sprouts and a zingy Asian dressing. Garnish with fresh coriander (cilantro), mint or Thai basil.

~~ Make a finely chopped salsa of avocado, tomato, cucumber and green chilli and spoon it over the schnitzel, or serve with a simple salad of tomato, olives, red onion and fresh oregano.

~~ In winter, a buttery mash is the perfect accompaniment to a crispy schnitzel along with steamed green beans, sautéed zucchini (courgette) or wilted English spinach.

Meatballs with fresh tomato sauce

I've used 'quick-cook oats' quite a few times in this book, and by that I mean the finer-textured oats that you can buy in the health food or cereal section of the supermarket, often called instant oats. I haven't called them instant oats in the recipes for fear that someone will open a sachet of honey-flavoured-just-add-boiling-water oats, as these really wouldn't work! You can use normal rolled oats, but their larger size makes them a bit more obvious, whereas the finer oats just meld into the meatball mixture.

125 ml (4 fl oz/½ cup) olive oil
1 brown onion, finely chopped
6 large ripe roma (plum) tomatoes, finely chopped
2 tablespoons tomato paste (concentrated purée)
350 g (12 oz) minced (ground) pork
150 g (5½ oz) minced (ground) veal or beef
25 g (1 oz/¼ cup) quick-cook rolled (porridge) oats
25 g (1 oz/¼ cup) finely grated parmesan cheese, plus extra to serve
2 tablespoons finely chopped flat-leaf (Italian) parsley
1 garlic clove, crushed
1 teaspoon finely grated lemon zest
2 teaspoons ground cumin
risoni or couscous, to serve
2 handfuls baby rocket (arugula) leaves

Heat 2 tablespoons of the olive oil in a large frying pan over medium heat and cook the onion for 5 minutes, or until softened and lightly browned. Add the tomatoes and tomato paste, reduce the heat to low, then cover the pan and simmer for 20 minutes, or until the tomato is soft and slightly broken down. Season with sea salt and freshly ground black pepper.

Meanwhile, put the pork and veal in a large bowl, then add the oats, parmesan, parsley, garlic, lemon zest, cumin and 2 tablespoons of the olive oil. Season with sea salt and freshly ground black pepper. Use your hands to combine all the ingredients together and then roll the pork mixture into bite-sized balls.

Heat the remaining olive oil in a large non-stick frying pan over medium heat. Cook the meatballs in batches for 8–10 minutes, or until lightly browned and cooked through. Pop the meatballs into the tomato sauce and simmer over low heat for 5 minutes.

Serve the meatballs and tomato sauce on a bed of risoni or couscous. Sprinkle with the extra parmesan and serve with rocket leaves.

SERVES 4

Whole baked snapper with tomato and avocado salad

In this recipe I cooked the fish in the oven, but there's no reason why you couldn't cook it in a covered barbecue. I say that because this really is a summer-time dish—fresh seafood, ripe tomatoes and fresh lemon and herb flavours—perfect for those lazy summer evenings outside, with a background chorus of cicadas and crickets.

1.5 kg (3 lb 5 oz) whole snapper
60 g (2¼ oz) butter, softened
1 lemon, halved
4 dill sprigs

TOMATO AND AVOCADO SALAD
400 g (14 oz/1 punnet) heirloom tomatoes (tomato medley), halved
2 celery stalks, sliced on the diagonal
25 g (1 oz/1 cup) celery leaves
1 teaspoon red wine vinegar
60 ml (2 fl oz/¼ cup) extra virgin olive oil
1 baby cos (romaine) lettuce, thickly sliced
2 avocados

Preheat the oven to 200°C (400°F). Pat the fish dry with paper towel. Using a sharp knife, score the fish in a crisscross pattern on both sides. Place two large sheets of foil on the work surface, ensuring that both pieces of foil are longer than the fish. Grease both sheets of foil with some of the softened butter, then place the fish on top of one sheet of foil.

Thinly slice one of the lemon halves and place the slices in the fish cavity, along with two of the dill sprigs. Squeeze the remaining lemon half over the fish and season with sea salt and freshly ground black pepper. Dab the remaining butter over the top of the fish and finely chop the remaining dill. Sprinkle the dill over the fish and then cover with the second sheet of foil. Fold the sides of the foil over to seal the fish within the foil. Place the wrapped fish on a large baking tray and pop it into the oven. Cook for 25 minutes.

Meanwhile, to make the tomato and avocado salad, put the tomatoes, celery, celery leaves, vinegar and olive oil in a bowl and season with sea salt and freshly ground black pepper. Toss to combine. Put the cos lettuce in a large serving bowl. Cut the avocados in half, remove the stones, then cut the flesh into thick chunks. Add the avocado to the bowl with the lettuce, spoon the tomato salad over the top, then drizzle with the dressing.

Remove the fish from the oven and open the foil. Check that the fish is cooked by pressing the tip of a knife into the thickest part of the flesh— the fish is cooked if it flakes easily and is no longer opaque.

Carefully transfer the fish to a large serving plate and spoon over any of the cooking juices. Serve with the salad.

SERVES 4

Barbecued steak with tomato and anchovy butter

This is not so much a recipe but a list of flavoured butters to enhance that eternal summer favourite, barbecued steak. I love the tomato and anchovy butter because it incorporates rich and smoky flavours with fresh parsley, but the tarragon and horseradish butter is a classic, and the wild mushroom option is perfect for a late-summer or autumn barbecue. The butters can be made in advance, rolled in baking paper and chilled until ready to use.

1 tablespoon olive oil
4 x 250 g (9 oz) beef sirloin steaks
1 teaspoon thyme leaves

TOMATO AND ANCHOVY BUTTER
2 ripe roma (plum) tomatoes
$^1/_2$ red onion, thickly sliced
3 anchovies, finely chopped
2 tablespoons finely chopped curly parsley
1 garlic clove, crushed
100 g (3$^1/_2$ oz) butter, softened

Preheat a barbecue grill or chargrill pan to medium–high. Rub the olive oil all over the steaks, then sprinkle with the thyme.

To make the tomato and anchovy butter, cut the tomatoes into quarters lengthways. Put the tomatoes and sliced onion on the hot grill and cook for about 5 minutes, or until they are slightly blackened all over. Remove to a clean board and coarsely chop. Transfer to a bowl and add the anchovies, parsley, garlic and butter. Season to taste with sea salt and freshly ground black pepper and stir to combine.

Cook the steaks on the hot grill for 3 minutes on each side, or until cooked to your liking. Remove to a warm plate and season to taste. Cover with foil and rest for 5 minutes.

Transfer the steaks to serving plates and spoon the butter mixture over the top. Serve with boiled new potatoes and dressed salad leaves.

SERVES 4

Other options:

TARRAGON AND HORSERADISH BUTTER
100 g (3^{1}/$_{2}$ oz) butter, softened
1 garlic clove, crushed
2 teaspoons finely chopped tarragon
2 tablespoons horseradish cream

Combine all the ingredients in a small bowl and season to taste.

WILD MUSHROOM BUTTER
10 g (^{1}/$_{4}$ oz) dried porcini mushrooms
125 ml (4 fl oz/^{1}/$_{2}$ cup) boiling water
100 g (3^{1}/$_{2}$ oz) butter, softened
^{1}/$_{4}$ brown onion, finely chopped
1 garlic clove, crushed

Put the porcini in a small bowl and pour over the boiling water. Set aside for 10 minutes, or until softened. Drain, reserving the soaking liquid, then finely chop the mushrooms.

Put 20 g (^{3}/$_{4}$ oz) of the butter in a small saucepan or frying pan and add the chopped mushrooms, onion and garlic. Cook for 5 minutes, or until the onion is soft and golden, then add the soaking liquid and season with sea salt and freshly ground black pepper. Continue to cook until the liquid has pretty much evaporated, then stir the mushroom mixture into the remaining butter.

Ocean trout and corn fritters

Here's a fishy twist on everyone's favourite, the corn fritter. You'll need a really sharp knife to chop the fish into a fine dice. If your knife skills aren't great, then wrap the fish fillet in plastic wrap and chill in the freezer for an hour. This will make the fish firmer and easier to slice and dice.

2 x 200 g (7 oz) boneless, skinless ocean trout fillets
3 corn cobs
7 g (1/4 oz/1/4 cup) finely chopped flat-leaf (Italian) parsley
130 g (4½ oz/1 cup) finely chopped leek (about 1 large leek), white part only
2 green chillies, seeded and finely chopped
75 g (2½ oz/½ cup) plain (all-purpose) flour
3 large free-range eggs, lightly beaten
80 ml (2½ fl oz/⅓ cup) vegetable oil

Preheat the oven to 140°C (275°F). Line a baking tray with baking paper.

Cut the trout fillets into a fine dice and place in a large bowl. Slice the corn kernels from the cobs and add them to the trout, then add the parsley, leek and chilli. Add the flour and mix until all the ingredients are lightly coated in the flour. Add the beaten egg and stir until the mixture comes together to form a thick batter.

Heat half of the oil in a large non-stick frying pan over medium–high heat. When the oil begins to shimmer, add heaped tablespoons of the trout mixture to the pan, lightly flattening the mix as you add it to the oil. Fry the fritters for 3–4 minutes on each side, or until golden brown. Transfer to the lined tray and keep warm in the oven. Repeat the process with the remaining oil and batter.

Serve the fritters with some mayonnaise and hot chilli sauce if desired, and a green salad.

SERVES 4

Maple roast chicken pieces

A healthier, home-cooked version of a fast-food favourite, this spicy roast chicken is served with sweet potato wedges and a bean salad. The chicken is finger-licking good and the sweet potato wedges work beautifully with the gingery flavours. The Tabasco sauce cuts the sweetness of the maple syrup and, because it's part of the marinade, it's not too hot. If you don't have any Tabasco, you can replace it with a teaspoon of red wine vinegar.

60 ml (2 fl oz/1/4 cup) maple syrup
2 tablespoons finely grated fresh ginger
1 tablespoon tomato paste (concentrated purée)
1 teaspoon Tabasco sauce
1 garlic clove, crushed
4 chicken Marylands (leg quarters)
600 g (1 lb 5 oz) orange sweet potato, cut into wedges

Put the maple syrup, ginger, tomato paste, Tabasco sauce and garlic in a large bowl and stir to combine. Add the chicken pieces and toss to coat in the marinade. Set aside for 30 minutes.

Preheat the oven to 180°C (350°F). Line a large baking tray with baking paper. Remove the chicken pieces from the marinade, reserving the marinade, and place on the lined tray. Nestle the sweet potato wedges around the chicken.

Roast the chicken pieces and sweet potato for 30 minutes, then remove the tray from the oven. Baste the chicken with the reserved marinade and turn the sweet potato wedges over. Return to the oven and bake for a further 20 minutes, or until the chicken is cooked through.

Serve the chicken with the sweet potato wedges and with a bean salad (page 184) or a mixed leaf salad.

SERVES 4

Pan-fried pork chops with cider cabbage

Ciders, both apple and pear, have been having a bit of a small brewery renaissance over the past few years, so I thought it would be nice to use some of these newer, full-bodied ciders in a simple pork dish. I've let the cider do all the talking here, but if you prefer a sweet, fruity accompaniment for your pork, then add a little grated apple or sliced pear to the cabbage.

50 g (1¾ oz) butter
½ teaspoon celery salt
500 g (1 lb 2 oz) Chinese cabbage (wong bok), thinly sliced
250 ml (9 fl oz/1 cup) apple cider
1 tablespoon olive oil
4 pork chops
1 small handful curly parsley, chopped

Preheat the oven to 180°C (350°F). Put the butter in a saucepan over medium–high heat and cook for 2–3 minutes, or until the butter begins to darken. Add the celery salt, cabbage and apple cider. Stir a few times, then reduce the heat to low, cover and cook for a further 5 minutes.

Meanwhile, preheat a barbecue plate or non-stick frying pan to medium. Rub the olive oil over the pork chops. When the barbecue or pan is hot, cook the chops for 2 minutes on each side. Transfer to a baking tray and cook in the oven for a further 8 minutes, or until cooked through.

Transfer the pork chops to four warmed serving plates and spoon the cabbage over the top. Sprinkle with the chopped parsley and serve with a side dish of buttery boiled new potatoes.

SERVES 4

Lamb skewers
with tzatziki

These lamb skewers have a lovely spiciness, and the tzatziki will tone down those flavours a little bit. Serve the skewers with a simple green salad, a Greek salad or some buttery couscous. And yes, you can buy the tzatziki, but it's so easy to make your own.

For this recipe you will need 12 medium metal skewers or wide bamboo skewers. If using bamboo skewers, soak them in water for an hour before using them, so they don't burn on the barbecue.

750 g (1 lb 10 oz) minced (ground) lamb
1 onion, grated
3 garlic cloves, crushed
2 teaspoons ground cumin
2 teaspoons ras el hanout
1/2 teaspoon ground cardamom
1 teaspoon ground ginger
1 teaspoon dried oregano
2 tablespoons olive oil
40 g (1 1/2 oz/1/4 cup) sesame seeds
lemon wedges, to serve

TZATZIKI
1 Lebanese (short) cucumber
1 teaspoon salt
1 garlic clove, crushed
260 g (9 1/4 oz/1 cup) Greek-style yoghurt
1/4 teaspoon ground white pepper

Combine the lamb, grated onion, garlic, cumin, ras el hanout, cardamom, ginger and oregano in a bowl and season with sea salt and freshly ground black pepper.

Take 2 heaped tablespoons of the lamb mixture and shape it into a long oval, then press it around one of the skewers. Repeat with the remaining mixture to make 12 skewers in total. Lightly brush the lamb skewers with the olive oil.

Preheat a barbecue grill or chargrill pan to medium. Sprinkle the sesame seeds over a plate and casually dip the lamb into the seeds, so as to haphazardly cover the lamb in the seeds. Cook the skewers, turning occasionally, for 10 minutes, or until the lamb is cooked through.

Meanwhile, to make the tzatziki, grate the cucumber into a bowl and add the salt. Leave for 10 minutes, then tip the cucumber (and any liquid) into a sieve. Using a spoon, press the cucumber against the sieve to remove all the excess liquid. Return the cucumber to the bowl and add the garlic, yoghurt and white pepper. Stir to combine. Serve the lamb skewers with the tzatziki, lemon wedges and a Greek salad.

SERVES 4

Seared salmon with 'gazpacho' salad

Sometimes ideas just come out of nowhere. I was writing a recipe for a gazpacho when it suddenly occurred to me how perfect all those flavours would be if combined with seafood. I love colourful diced salsas spooned over freshly grilled fish, so it wasn't hard to jump to the idea of a gazpacho salsa. It's worthwhile investing in a good-quality sherry vinegar for the salsa, but if you can't find one, use a good-quality red wine vinegar instead.

2 vine-ripened tomatoes, finely diced
1 Lebanese (short) cucumber, finely diced
1 red capsicum (pepper), finely diced
1 green capsicum (pepper), finely diced
1/4 red onion, finely diced
1 garlic clove, crushed
1/4 teaspoon smoked paprika
1 tablespoon sherry vinegar
2 tablespoons extra virgin olive oil
4 x 200 g (7 oz) salmon steaks (cutlets)
lemon wedges, to serve

Combine the tomato, cucumber, red and green capsicum, onion, garlic, paprika, vinegar and olive oil in a bowl. Season generously with sea salt and freshly ground black pepper and toss to combine.

Preheat a barbecue grill or chargrill pan to medium–high. Cook the salmon steaks on the hot barbecue for about 3 minutes on each side, or until cooked to your liking.

Transfer the salmon to four warmed plates and spoon over the gazpacho salad. Serve with the lemon wedges and, if desired, some buttery boiled new potatoes or crispy garlic bread.

SERVES 4

Lamb leg roast
with nutty mash

I always joke that I
must have been Irish
in a previous life
because I never tire of
potatoes, no matter how
they are cooked. Let's
face it, the potato is both
terrifyingly adaptable
and delicious—my
waistline says 'stop' but
my heart says 'just dive
in'. Here I've used the
humble potato to make
a skordalia-inspired
mashed potato, laced
with lots of garlic,
chopped parsley and
toasted almonds.

30 g (1 oz) flaked almonds
2 rosemary sprigs
1 small boned lamb leg (ready-rolled lamb roast) (about 1 kg/2 lb 4 oz)
1 tablespoon olive oil
600 g (1 lb 5 oz) all-purpose potatoes, such as desiree, peeled and cut
    into chunks
4 garlic cloves, peeled
finely grated zest and juice of 1 lemon
80 ml (2½ fl oz/⅓ cup) extra virgin olive oil
1 handful flat-leaf (Italian) parsley leaves, finely chopped
lemon wedges, to serve

Preheat the oven to 200°C (400°F). Put the almonds on a baking tray and cook in the oven for a few minutes, or until lightly golden, taking care as they can burn quickly. Remove from the oven and set aside to cool.

Put the rosemary sprigs in the base of a roasting tin. Sit the lamb on top of the rosemary, then rub the olive oil all over the lamb. Season with sea salt and a little freshly ground black pepper. Place the lamb in the oven and roast for 1 hour 10 minutes, or until medium-rare.

Meanwhile, put the potatoes and garlic in a saucepan filled with salted, cold water. Bring to the boil and cook for 15 minutes, or until the potatoes are cooked through. Drain the potatoes and garlic, reserving some of the cooking liquid, then return them to the warm saucepan. Add the lemon zest, lemon juice and extra virgin olive oil and mash until smooth and creamy, adding some of the reserved water if necessary. Stir through the toasted almonds and chopped parsley and season to taste.

Remove the lamb roast from the oven and transfer to a warm plate. Cover with foil and rest for 5 minutes. Slice the lamb and serve with the mashed potato and lemon wedges, and with minty peas or a green salad.

SERVES 4

Sticky chicken thighs with fried onion rice

Sweet, sticky chicken and fried rice ... what's not to like! I've kept this fried rice quite simple, just using various versions of the onion, but feel free to add some herbs or any vegetables that you've found lurking in the bottom of the fridge that are crying out to be used. This is one of those dishes that will happily accept all newcomers.

60 ml (2 fl oz/¼ cup) olive oil
2 tablespoons dijon mustard
80 ml (2½ fl oz/⅓ cup) Worcestershire sauce
1 tablespoon tomato paste (concentrated purée)
90 g (3¼ oz/¼ cup) honey
1 lemon, juiced
4 boneless, skinless chicken thigh fillets
1 onion, thinly sliced
4 spring onions (scallions), white part only, thinly sliced
1 tablespoon soy sauce
370 g (13 oz/2 cups) cooked long-grain rice
20 g (¾ oz/1 bunch) chives, finely snipped

Put 1 tablespoon of the olive oil in a large bowl with the mustard, Worcestershire sauce, tomato paste, honey and lemon juice. Stir to combine, then add the chicken thighs and toss to coat them in the marinade. Cover with plastic wrap and refrigerate for 2 hours.

Preheat the oven to 180°C (350°F). Line a roasting tin with baking paper. Transfer the chicken to the tin and roast for 10–15 minutes, basting occasionally, until the chicken is cooked through.

Meanwhile, heat the remaining 2 tablespoons of olive oil in a large frying pan over medium heat and fry the onion and spring onion for 10 minutes, or until well caramelised and quite dark in colour. Add the soy sauce, then the rice and chives and stir until well combined. Serve the chicken with the fried rice and a green salad.

SERVES 4

Fish parcels with roast vegetables

For some reason, a lot of people are nervous about cooking fish. If that sounds like you, then I encourage you to give this recipe a go as it's so quick and easy—and pretty much foolproof. The fish is steamed in paper parcels, which keeps it perfectly moist, and the roast vegetables and olives are a delicious accompaniment.

800 g (1 lb 12 oz) waxy potatoes, peeled
1 large fennel bulb (450 g/1 lb)
4 garlic cloves, bruised
250 g (9 oz/1 punnet) cherry tomatoes
16 kalamata olives
2 tablespoons olive oil
4 x 150 g (5½ oz) boneless, skinless firm white fish fillets
2 lemons, 1 thinly sliced and 1 cut into wedges
4 teaspoons butter

Preheat the oven to 200°C (400°F). Cut the potatoes and fennel into 3 cm (1¼ inch) chunks, reserving the fennel fronds for later.

Put the potatoes, fennel, garlic cloves, tomatoes and olives in a bowl. Add the olive oil and season with sea salt and freshly ground black pepper. Toss to combine, then put the seasoned vegetables on a roasting tray and roast in the oven for 30 minutes.

Meanwhile, take four large sheets of baking paper and wet each piece under some running water to soften it. Place a piece of fish in the centre of each sheet of paper. Top each fish with two slices of lemon, some of the fennel fronds and 1 teaspoon of the butter. Season well, then wrap up the paper parcels, enclosing the fish.

When the vegetables have been in the oven for 30 minutes and the potatoes are lightly golden, put the fish parcels on a separate baking tray and bake for 15 minutes. After this time, both the fish and vegetables should be cooked through. Remove the fish parcels from the oven and unwrap one. Press the tip of a knife into the thickest part of the flesh—the fish is cooked if it flakes easily and is no longer opaque.

Serve the fish parcels with the roast vegetables and lemon wedges. You can also serve the fish with green sauce (page 142) or lemon–mustard mayonnaise (page 166).

SERVES 4

Sticky ribs with spiced corn

This meal is all about the sticky, succulent ribs and buttery spiced corn and is perfect for the family that loves a meal that's both spicy and messy! If you prefer a meal with a little less spice, then serve the ribs with creamy mashed potato and save the buttery jalapeño corn for another meal with more subdued flavours.

2 kg (4 lb 8 oz) American-style pork spare ribs
4 corn cobs

MARINADE
60 ml (2 fl oz/¼ cup) cider vinegar
60 ml (2 fl oz/¼ cup) maple syrup
60 ml (2 fl oz/¼ cup) soy sauce
2 garlic cloves, crushed
80 ml (2½ fl oz/⅓ cup) tomato paste (concentrated purée)
1 tablespoon finely grated orange zest
1 tablespoon dijon mustard
1 tablespoon finely grated fresh ginger
½ teaspoon ground cumin
¼ teaspoon chilli powder

SPICED BUTTER
100 g (3½ oz) salted butter, softened
1 tablespoon finely chopped bottled jalapeño peppers
1 tablespoon finely chopped coriander (cilantro) leaves
¼ teaspoon sweet paprika

To make the marinade for the ribs, put all the ingredients in a small saucepan and bring to the boil, stirring to ensure the marinade does not catch on the base of the pan. When everything is well combined, remove from the heat and set aside to cool.

Put the pork ribs in a large storage container. Pour the marinade over the ribs, then turn the ribs in the marinade to ensure they are well coated. Cover and refrigerate for several hours, or preferably overnight.

Preheat the oven to 180°C (350°F). Line a baking tray with baking paper and add the ribs. Pour any remaining marinade over the top, then cover with foil. Roast for 20 minutes, then remove the foil and baste the ribs with some of the marinade and juices on the base of the tray. Roast for a further 40 minutes, uncovered, turning the ribs over after 20 minutes.

Meanwhile, to make the spiced butter for the corn, combine the softened butter in a bowl with the jalapeño, coriander and paprika. Stir to combine.

Bring a large saucepan of salted water to the boil and cook the corn cobs for 5 minutes, then drain.

Transfer the corn to a serving platter and spoon the spiced butter over the cobs. Remove the ribs from the oven and transfer to a second serving platter. Serve with a green salad and lime wedges.

SERVES 4

Cottage pie

I almost didn't include this recipe because I wondered if anyone needed a recipe for savoury mince, but it's such a golden oldie and always a family favourite that, in the end, I decided it was a must. As a little twist, I've topped the cottage pie with thin rounds of potato, but if your nostalgic heart runs to buttery mash or a grated cheese topping, then by all means go with tradition. And if there are any leftovers, reheated savoury mince on toast will always make the heart sing on a cold day.

2 tablespoons olive oil
2 onions, finely chopped
2 celery stalks, finely chopped
2 garlic cloves, crushed
500 g (1 lb 2 oz) minced (ground) beef
2 carrots, peeled and grated
2 zucchini (courgettes), grated
250 ml (9 fl oz/1 cup) vegetable stock
400 g (14 oz) tinned diced tomatoes
1/2 teaspoon finely chopped rosemary
2 fresh bay leaves
2 large (600 g/1 lb 5 oz) all-purpose potatoes, such as desiree
50 g (1 3/4 oz) butter, melted
1 small handful thyme sprigs

Preheat the oven to 200°C (400°F). Heat 1 tablespoon of the olive oil in a large frying pan over medium heat. Add the onion and celery and fry for 3–4 minutes, or until lightly browned, then add the garlic and cook for 1 minute. Increase the heat to high, add the beef and cook, stirring, for 8–10 minutes, or until browned.

Add the carrot, zucchini, stock, tomatoes, rosemary and bay leaves. Bring to a simmer and cook, uncovered, for about 30 minutes, or until all the liquid has evaporated and the meat sauce is thick. Remove from the heat.

Meanwhile, peel the potatoes and put them in a ceramic dish. Cover and microwave for 3 minutes on High (100%). Remove and set aside to cool.

Remove the bay leaves from the meat sauce and season to taste with sea salt and freshly ground black pepper. Spoon the meat sauce into a 1.5 litre (52 fl oz/6 cup) ovenproof dish and smooth the top.

Thinly slice the potatoes and arrange them over the top of the meat sauce. Brush with the melted butter and sprinkle with the thyme sprigs. Cover with a piece of baking paper, then a piece of foil pressed around the side of the dish to hold the paper in place and seal the dish. Bake for 15 minutes, then remove the foil and baking paper and bake for a further 20 minutes, or until browned.

SERVES 4

Moroccan chicken pies

It does take a little more time to make this recipe than the others but it's definitely worth it, and you can always make the chicken filling ahead of time. You can have lots of fun with the filo pastry topping by scrunching it, rippling it, slicing thin lines into it, sprinkling it with sesame seeds or just simply laying it over the filling.

500 g (1 lb 2 oz) boneless, skinless chicken thigh fillets
2 tablespoons plain (all-purpose) flour
1 teaspoon ground cumin
2 tablespoons olive oil
75 g (2¹/₂ oz/1 small bunch) coriander (cilantro), rinsed well
1 leek, white part only, rinsed and thinly sliced
2 carrots, peeled and diced
1 green chilli, seeded and thinly sliced
250 ml (9 fl oz/1 cup) chicken stock
2 teaspoons finely chopped preserved lemon rind
6 sheets filo pastry
50 g (1³/₄ oz) butter, melted
1 tablespoon zaatar
1–2 teaspoons sesame seeds

Cut the chicken thighs into small bite-sized pieces. Put the flour and cumin in a clean plastic bag and season with sea salt and freshly ground black pepper. Add the chicken pieces to the bag and toss to coat in the seasoned flour.

Heat the olive oil in a large frying pan over medium heat and fry the chicken pieces for 5 minutes, or until golden all over. You will need to do this in batches, setting the pieces to one side as they are cooked.

Finely chop the roots and stems of the coriander and add to the pan, along with the leek, carrot and chilli. Cook for 3–4 minutes, or until the leek is soft, then return the chicken to the pan. Add the stock and bring to the boil, then reduce the heat to a simmer. Cook for 30 minutes, uncovered, or until the mixture is quite thick and reduced.

Remove from the heat and stir through the preserved lemon and some roughly chopped coriander leaves. Spoon the mixture into four individual pie dishes or 250 ml (9 fl oz/1 cup) ramekins or ovenproof bowls.

Preheat the oven to 200°C (400°F). Put one sheet of filo pastry on a clean chopping board and brush with some of the melted butter. Sprinkle a little zaatar over the top of the filo, then cover with another sheet of filo. Repeat the process with the remaining filo, butter and zaatar. If simply covering the pie, cut the filo into four rounds, slightly larger than the pie dishes. Place the filo rounds on top of each chicken pie, tucking the filo in around the edges. If scrunching or rippling the pastry, then simply cut the pastry into four pieces and roughly arrange it over the top of the mixture. Brush with a little butter and sprinkle some sesame seeds over the top of each pie.

Bake for 20 minutes, or until the pastry is golden brown. Serve the chicken pies with steamed green beans or a salad.

SERVES 4

one pot

Red wine beef with dumplings

I've always had a fondness for dumplings and it's not because when I was a child I could have been described as one. Don't mock—I have photographic proof!

Nobody seems to make old-fashioned dumplings anymore. In fact, nowadays if you mention dumplings people instantly think of yum cha but, on cold wintery nights, there really is nothing more warming than a buttery dumpling soaked in a rich, meaty sauce.

1 kg (2 lb 4 oz) stewing beef
60 ml (2 fl oz/1/4 cup) olive oil
350 g (12 oz) pancetta, diced
2 garlic cloves, finely chopped
1 carrot, peeled and cut into chunks
2 celery stalks, sliced
400 g (14 oz) tinned chopped tomatoes
500 ml (17 fl oz/2 cups) red wine
2 fresh bay leaves
12 baby onions, peeled

DUMPLINGS
150 g (5^{1}/$_{2}$ oz/1 cup) plain (all-purpose) flour
1 tablespoon finely chopped curly parsley, plus extra to serve
pinch of salt
70 g (2^{1}/$_{2}$ oz) chilled butter, diced

Trim the beef and cut it into bite-sized pieces. Heat the olive oil in a large heavy-based saucepan or flameproof casserole dish over medium heat. Add the pancetta and cook for 2 minutes, or until the pancetta is golden and crispy. Remove the pancetta with a slotted spoon, leaving the oil in the saucepan, and set to one side.

Increase the heat to high and cook the beef in batches until browned all over. Return the pancetta to the saucepan and add the garlic, carrot, celery, tomatoes, wine, bay leaves and onions. Cover, then reduce the heat to low and simmer for 1 hour.

Meanwhile, make the dumplings. Put the flour and parsley in a bowl with a pinch of salt. Using your fingertips, rub the butter into the flour until the mixture resembles breadcrumbs. Add 1 tablespoon of cold water and work it into the dough with a knife. Try to handle the dough as little as possible. Gather the dough into eight small lumps and loosely roll into balls.

After the beef stew has cooked for 1 hour, drop the dumplings into the stew and continue to simmer, covered, for a further 25 minutes. Serve the stew and dumplings garnished with extra chopped parsley and a side dish of steamed green beans.

SERVES 4

Gran's spring chicken casserole

When we were young, and whenever we were sick, my grandmother would make this dish for us. It was her somewhat heartier version of chicken soup. To this day I still make this casserole whenever I'm in need of a generous dose of comforting soul food.

2 tablespoons plain (all-purpose) flour
1 tablespoon ground cumin
4 chicken Marylands (leg quarters)
2 tablespoons olive oil
2 leeks, white part only, rinsed and cut into 2 cm (3/4 inch) rounds
2 large carrots, peeled and cut into chunks
2 celery stalks, cut into 2 cm (3/4 inch) lengths
350 g (12 oz) kipfler (fingerling) potatoes, scrubbed and cut into chunks
1 rosemary sprig
1 fresh bay leaf
4 thyme sprigs
250 ml (9 fl oz/1 cup) dry white wine
250 ml (9 fl oz/1 cup) chicken stock
1 handful flat-leaf (Italian) parsley leaves, roughly chopped

---

Preheat the oven to 180°C (350°F). Put the flour and cumin in a plastic bag or large snaplock bag and season with sea salt and freshly ground black pepper. Add the chicken pieces to the bag and toss to coat lightly in the seasoned flour.

Heat the olive oil in a large flameproof casserole dish over medium heat and fry the chicken pieces for 2–3 minutes on each side, or until they are lightly golden. Remove the chicken from the casserole dish, then remove the dish from the heat.

Place half of the vegetables in the casserole dish along with the fresh herbs, wine and stock. Arrange the chicken on top of the vegetables and then add the remaining vegetables.

Cover the dish with a lid and cook in the oven for 1 hour, or until the chicken is cooked through. Scatter with chopped parsley and serve.

SERVES 4

Sausage and barley casserole

Here is an easy, child-friendly meal that seems to appeal to nearly everyone. It's hearty, it's simple and, with the wide range of sausages available these days from both butchers and supermarkets, you can adjust the flavour a little according to your choice of sausage.

5 ripe roma (plum) tomatoes, roughly chopped
400 g (14 oz) tinned chopped tomatoes
2 celery stalks, sliced
1 carrot, peeled and diced
2 leeks, white part only, rinsed and finely chopped
4 garlic cloves, crushed
1 teaspoon thyme leaves
1 teaspoon rosemary leaves
250 ml (9 fl oz/1 cup) white wine
100 g (3^1/$_2$ oz/^{1}/$_2$ cup) pearl barley
350 g (12 oz) good-quality spicy, thick sausages
15 g (^{1}/$_2$ oz/^{1}/$_2$ cup) roughly chopped flat-leaf (Italian) parsley

---

Preheat the oven to 180°C (350°F). Put the fresh and tinned tomatoes in a flameproof casserole dish, along with the celery, carrot, leek, garlic, thyme, rosemary, wine and barley.

Prick the skins of the sausages with a fork and then sear them in a frying pan over high heat until they are browned all over.

Cut the sausages into bite-sized pieces and add them to the casserole dish. Pour in 250 ml (9 fl oz/1 cup) water and gently stir everything together. Cover with a lid and cook in the oven for 1^1/$_2$ hours. Scatter with the chopped parsley and serve with warm crusty bread.

SERVES 4–6

Bacon and tomato risotto

When it comes to risotto, it seems that people fall into one of two camps: those who love making risottos and those who think they involve too much stirring. To the second group of people, I say turn to page 98 for the baked risotto recipe. However, if you are in the first group, let's all agree that once you get the hang of a risotto, they are one of the easiest dishes to cook. Not only that, but there is actually something quite lovely about standing at the stove with a glass of wine in one hand and a spoon in the other, stirring a risotto into life.

1 litre (35 fl oz/4 cups) chicken stock
40 g (1½ oz) butter
1 leek, white part only, rinsed and finely chopped
2 garlic cloves, finely chopped
4 rindless bacon rashers, diced
330 g (11½ oz/1½ cups) arborio rice
1 tablespoon tomato paste (concentrated purée)
125 ml (4 fl oz/½ cup) white wine
3 ripe roma (plum) tomatoes, diced
50 g (2 oz/½ cup) finely grated parmesan cheese
extra virgin olive oil, to serve
small basil leaves, to serve

Bring the stock to the boil in a saucepan, then reduce the heat to very low to keep the stock at a low simmer.

Put the butter in a large saucepan over medium heat, then add the leek, garlic and bacon and cook, stirring, for 5 minutes, or until the leek is soft and transparent. Add the rice and stir for 1 minute, or until the grains are well coated and glossy.

Ladle 250 ml (9 fl oz/1 cup) of the hot stock into the pan with the rice, then add the tomato paste and wine. Simmer, stirring, until the liquid is completely absorbed. Add another 250 ml (9 fl oz/1 cup) of stock and the diced tomato. Cook, stirring, for a few more minutes until the stock has completely absorbed, then add another 250 ml (9 fl oz/1 cup) of stock. Cook until all the liquid has been absorbed, then test the rice to see if it is *al dente*. If it needs more cooking, add the remaining stock.

Add half of the parmesan and gently fold it into the risotto. Spoon into four warmed pasta bowls and sprinkle with the remaining parmesan. Drizzle with a little extra virgin olive oil and scatter with the basil leaves.

SERVES 4

Spiced lamb

This is a richly aromatic lamb stew that's similar in style to a tagine, but without the added sweetness of fruit. I've teamed it with a toasted almond gremolata, which brings a bit of crunch to the dish, a texture I always crave when eating meaty, stewy meals.

80 ml (2^1/$_2$ fl oz/^{1}/$_3$ cup) olive oil
1 kg (2 lb 4 oz) boned lamb shoulder, cubed
1 onion, thinly sliced
1 teaspoon ground ginger
1 teaspoon saffron threads
1 teaspoon ground coriander
2 garlic cloves, thinly sliced
1 celery stalk, thinly sliced
2 carrots, peeled and roughly chopped
3 roma (plum) tomatoes, peeled and chopped
250 ml (9 fl oz/1 cup) vegetable stock
1 tablespoon finely chopped flat-leaf (Italian) parsley
300 g (10^1/$_2$ oz) green beans, trimmed

ALMOND GREMOLATA
1 large red chilli, seeded and thinly sliced
50 g (1^3/$_4$ oz/^{1}/$_2$ cup) flaked almonds, lightly toasted
2^1/$_2$ tablespoons finely chopped flat-leaf (Italian) parsley
1 tablespoon finely grated lemon zest

Heat 2 tablespoons of the olive oil in a large flameproof casserole dish or large heavy-based saucepan over medium heat. Add the lamb in batches and cook until browned all over. Transfer the lamb pieces to a plate as they are browned.

Heat the remaining olive oil in the casserole dish and add the onion, ginger, saffron, coriander and garlic. Cook, stirring, for several minutes, or until the spices are fragrant and the onion is lightly golden.

Return the lamb to the dish, along with the celery, carrot and tomato, and cook for 5 minutes, or until the vegetables are tender. Add the stock and parsley and bring to the boil. Reduce the heat to low, cover the dish with a lid and simmer for 40 minutes, then remove the lid and cook, uncovered, for a further 40 minutes. Add the green beans to the dish, cover and cook for a further 5 minutes.

Meanwhile, to make the almond gremolata, put all the ingredients in a bowl and stir to combine.

Ladle the lamb stew into shallow bowls and serve topped with spoonfuls of the almond gremolata. For a heartier meal, serve with steamed couscous on the side.

SERVES 6

Spinach and ricotta cannelloni

Comforting and rich, this is the perfect meal for wintery evenings. The spinach and cheese filling is an old favourite and the olive-studded tomato sauce cuts through the richness of the cheese, making it a winner for everyone. Like lasagne, cannelloni reheats well, so it's worth making a weekend batch that will fill hungry post-match tummies.

The ricotta filling makes a great base for a summery cheese and spinach pie—just add finely chopped fresh mint and chives to the mixture and sandwich it between layers of buttery filo.

SAUCE
2 tablespoons olive oil
1 onion, finely chopped
2 garlic cloves
400 ml (14 fl oz) tomato passata
10 basil leaves, thinly sliced
10 pitted black olives, roughly chopped
1 zucchini (courgette), finely diced

FILLING
250 g (9 oz) frozen spinach, thawed
400 g (14 oz) fresh full-fat ricotta cheese
100 g (3½ oz) feta cheese, crumbled
3 spring onions (scallions), thinly sliced
7 g (¼ oz/¼ cup) finely chopped flat-leaf (Italian) parsley
80 g (2¾ oz/¾ cup) finely grated parmesan cheese

12 cannelloni tubes

Preheat the oven to 180°C (350°F). First find a baking dish that will comfortably fit the cannelloni in one layer—we used an 18 x 25 cm (7 x 10 inch) dish. Generously grease the dish with butter.

To make the sauce, heat the olive oil in a frying pan over medium heat and cook the onion and garlic for 3–4 minutes, or until the onion is lightly golden. Add the passata, basil, olives and zucchini and cook for a further 5 minutes.

Meanwhile, to make the filling, squeeze the spinach to remove the excess liquid. Put it in a bowl with the ricotta, feta, spring onion, parsley and half of the parmesan. Stir to combine. Fill the cannelloni tubes with the spinach and ricotta mixture and then lay them, side by side, in the baking dish.

Season the tomato sauce and then spoon the sauce over the cannelloni. Bake in the oven for 30 minutes, then remove from the oven and sprinkle the remaining parmesan over the top. Return to the oven and cook for a further 15 minutes, or until the cheese is golden and bubbling. Serve with a green salad.

SERVES 4

Mussels with tomato and chorizo

I always think of a bowl of mussels as a meal divided into two quite separate experiences. The first is all about the glossy-shelled mussels and their succulent meat. The second is all about the broth at the bottom of your bowl, which cries out for a big chunk of buttery, crusty bread to soak up the wonderful juices. This is definitely a meal to be eaten with great gusto!

2 kg (4 lb 8 oz) mussels
2 tablespoons extra virgin olive oil
1 onion, diced
4 garlic cloves, finely chopped
1 small carrot, peeled and diced
1 celery stalk, finely chopped
1/2 fennel bulb (about 150 g/51/2 oz), diced
2 ripe roma (plum) tomatoes, diced
70 g (21/2 oz) chorizo sausage, finely chopped
250 ml (9 fl oz/1 cup) dry white wine
1 tablespoon finely chopped curly parsley

Clean the mussels under cold running water, scrubbing them to remove any barnacles or bits of hairy beard. Discard any broken mussels or open ones that don't close when tapped on the kitchen bench. Rinse well.

Heat the olive oil in a large saucepan over medium heat. Add the onion, garlic, carrot, celery, fennel, tomato and chorizo and sauté for 5 minutes, or until the vegetables are tender.

Increase the heat to high and add the wine and mussels. Cover the pan and cook for 1 minute, shaking the pan. Remove the lid and use kitchen tongs to remove the mussels that have opened, transferring them to a large bowl. Cover the pan again and cook for a further 1 minute, to cook any mussels that have not yet opened.

Divide the mussels and broth among four large bowls. Sprinkle with the parsley and serve with warm crusty bread.

SERVES 4

Prawn curry

The only difficult thing about making this curry is finding the required spices in your cupboard. Once you have them all lined up, the actual curry takes no time at all and will fill the house with the most delicious aromas. It's a quick and easy midweek curry fix, especially if you have your spices alphabetically arranged!

80 ml (2½ fl oz/⅓ cup) vegetable oil
2 onions, finely chopped
4 garlic cloves, finely chopped
3 tablespoons finely grated fresh ginger
½ teaspoon ground turmeric
½ teaspoon ground cumin
1 teaspoon garam masala
¼ teaspoon cayenne pepper
500 ml (17 fl oz/2 cups) vegetable stock
5 ripe tomatoes, chopped
24 raw king prawns (jumbo shrimp), peeled and deveined, tails left intact
1 lime, quartered

Heat the oil in a deep-sided frying pan over medium heat and add the onion, garlic, ginger, turmeric, cumin, garam masala and cayenne pepper. Cook, stirring occasionally, for 10 minutes, or until the onion is soft and the spices are fragrant.

Add the stock and tomatoes and cook for a further 15 minutes, or until the liquid has reduced and thickened a little. Add the prawns and cook for 3 minutes, or until they are just cooked through.

Spoon the spicy prawns into shallow bowls and serve with the lime wedges and some naan bread or saffron rice.

SERVES 4

Baked risotto

For those of us who don't like to stand and stir, this is an easy quick-mix approach to risotto. It probably shouldn't be called a risotto, and I'm sure the purists will be horrified at the thought, but somehow 'baked savoury rice' just doesn't have the same appeal—that sounds like some awful concoction served in old boarding school dining halls, whereas this is a comforting scoop of warm, cheesy Italian flavours.

80 ml (2½ fl oz/⅓ cup) olive oil
1 onion, finely chopped
2 garlic cloves, crushed
200 g (7 oz) pancetta, finely diced
1 teaspoon thyme leaves
1 medium eggplant (aubergine), about 300 g (10½ oz), diced
1 red capsicum (pepper), about 300 g (10½ oz), diced
220 g (7¾ oz/1 cup) arborio rice
750 ml (26 fl oz/3 cups) vegetable stock
1 teaspoon finely grated lemon zest
3 bocconcini (fresh baby mozzarella cheese), about 80 g (2¾ oz), chopped
50 g (1¾ oz/½ cup) finely grated parmesan cheese

Preheat the oven to 200°C (400°F). You will need a large flameproof casserole dish, about 1.5 litres (52 fl oz/6 cups) in capacity.

Heat the olive oil in the casserole dish over medium heat. Add the onion, garlic, pancetta and thyme and cook for 3–4 minutes, or until the onion is soft and golden. Add the eggplant and cook for 3 minutes, stirring to ensure that it cooks evenly.

Add the capsicum and rice to the dish and stir for 1 minute before adding the stock and lemon zest. Season with freshly ground black pepper. Stir once to combine, then cover with the lid, transfer to the oven and bake for 30 minutes.

Remove the dish from the oven and scatter the chopped bocconcini and grated parmesan over the top. Return to the oven and cook, uncovered, for a further 10 minutes. Serve with a green salad.

SERVES 4–6

Chicken with green olives and artichokes

If you are lucky enough to have an Italian grandmother, this recipe would be typical home-style comfort food, but both my grandmothers were Scottish, so for us it was all oats, barley and braises! I'm now making up for lost time, and a slightly stodgy heritage, by spending hungry hours plotting and planning in Italian delis.

2 leeks, white part only, rinsed and sliced into 1 cm (1/2 inch) rounds
1 celery stalk, chopped
500 g (1 lb 2 oz) waxy potatoes, such as kipfler (fingerling), scrubbed
    and cut into 4 cm (1 1/2 inch) chunks
500 ml (17 fl oz/2 cups) chicken or vegetable stock
1 tablespoon lemon juice
1 fresh bay leaf
4 chicken Marylands (leg quarters)
16 marinated artichoke quarters
16 large green olives
4 prosciutto slices

Preheat the oven to 180°C (350°F). Put the chopped leeks, celery and potatoes in a large roasting dish and add the stock, lemon juice and bay leaf. Arrange the chicken pieces over the top of the vegetables and cover with foil. Roast in the oven for 40 minutes.

Remove the dish from the oven and add the artichokes and olives, then lay the prosciutto slices over the chicken and roast, uncovered, for a further 20 minutes, or until the chicken is crisp and golden on top.

Serve the chicken with the vegetables and broth and, if you like, a large spoonful of green sauce (page 142).

SERVES 4

You can use any cooked artichoke for this recipe: home-made (if you're lucky), bottled or, preferably, the chargrilled artichoke halves you can sometimes buy from the antipasto section in the supermarket.

Fish stew

For this spicy fish stew I've chosen to serve the coconut cream on the side rather than cooking it into the dish, as I find the coconut cream can diffuse the flavours a little. I love the richness of this stew, and the peppery flavours work so beautifully with the fish. So, spoon the coconut cream over the stew after you've served it and enjoy both tropical and earthy flavours in the one mouthful.

2 tablespoons olive oil
1 tablespoon ground cumin
1 tablespoon ground turmeric
1/2 teaspoon ground white pepper
1 leek, white part only, rinsed and finely chopped
1 garlic clove, crushed
1 large red chilli, seeded and finely chopped
2 large ripe tomatoes, cut into 1 cm (1/2 inch) cubes
800 g (1 lb 12 oz) tinned diced tomatoes
2 tablespoons light brown sugar
1 green capsicum (pepper), cut into 1 cm (1/2 inch) cubes
100 g (31/2 oz/1/2 cup) jasmine rice
800 g (1 lb 12 oz) firm, white-fleshed fish, cut into chunks
1 handful coriander (cilantro) sprigs
1 lime, quartered
160 ml (51/4 fl oz) coconut cream

Heat the olive oil in a large heavy-based frying pan over medium heat and add the cumin, turmeric, white pepper, leek and garlic. Stir until the spices are fragrant and the leek is soft and golden.

Add the chilli, fresh and tinned tomatoes, brown sugar, capsicum, rice and 1 litre (35 fl oz/4 cups) water. Bring to the boil, then reduce the heat and simmer for 30 minutes. Season to taste with sea salt and freshly ground black pepper. Add the fish, then cover the pan and cook for a further 10 minutes, or until the fish is cooked.

Divide the fish stew among four warmed bowls. Scatter with coriander sprigs and serve with the lime wedges. Serve the coconut cream on the side, to drizzle over the top.

SERVES 4

Roast carrot soup with sesame salt

I discovered this sesame salt a few years ago when I was doing some research on Korean cooking. I came across a recipe for a simmered chicken that was served with the salt. It was delicious—delicious on the chicken, delicious on green vegetables and delicious sprinkled over steamed rice. Needless to say, whenever I make it, I always make a double batch.

This is a very simple carrot soup that is sweetened and enriched by roasting the vegetables first—although it's the sesame salt that really takes this soup to a new level. I've used carrots here, but the recipe would work just as well with roast pumpkin.

1 kg (2 lb 4 oz) carrots, peeled and cut into chunks
1 leek, white part only, rinsed and cut into 2 cm (³/4 inch) pieces
4 garlic cloves, peeled
2 tablespoons olive oil
1 litre (35 fl oz/4 cups) vegetable stock
1 small handful coriander (cilantro) leaves

SESAME SALT
2 tablespoons sesame seeds
1 teaspoon sea salt

Preheat the oven to 180°C (350°F). Put the carrot, leek and garlic cloves in a roasting tin. Add the olive oil and toss to coat. Season with sea salt and freshly ground black pepper. Cover the tin with foil and roast for 1¹/2 hours.

Meanwhile, to make the sesame salt, put the sesame seeds in a small frying pan over low heat and cook, stirring constantly, until the seeds start to turn golden brown. Transfer the seeds to a mortar and pestle and add the salt. Work the sesame seeds and salt together until the seeds are slightly broken down.

Remove the vegetables from the oven and transfer to a food processor. Blend until smooth, then tip the carrot purée into a saucepan and add the stock. Bring to the boil, stirring to combine.

Ladle the carrot soup into four bowls. Sprinkle with the sesame salt and coriander leaves.

SERVES 4

Green curry lamb shanks

Lamb shanks always make me think of winter and, to be honest, it's the only time I really feel like cooking them. With that in mind, I thought it might be nice to bring some summery flavours to this wintery dish. I've given the shanks an Asian twist with Thai green curry paste, ginger, coconut milk and a scattering of fresh coriander.

80 ml (2½ fl oz/⅓ cup) olive oil
4 lamb shanks (1 kg/2 lb 4 oz in total)
3 brown onions, sliced
2 tablespoons green curry paste
1 tablespoon finely grated fresh ginger
1 tablespoon ground turmeric
90 g (3¼ oz/1 bunch) coriander (cilantro), rinsed well
270 ml (9½ fl oz) coconut milk
500 g (1 lb 2 oz) baby kipfler (fingerling) potatoes, scrubbed and halved
300 g (10½ oz) green beans, trimmed and halved lengthways
2 tablespoons lemon juice

Heat 2 tablespoons of the olive oil in a large flameproof casserole dish or deep-sided frying pan over high heat and cook the lamb shanks until browned all over. Transfer the shanks to a plate lined with paper towel to drain.

Heat the remaining oil in the casserole dish over medium heat and add the onion, curry paste, ginger and turmeric. Finely chop the roots and stems of the coriander and add them to the onion, stirring to combine. Cook for 5 minutes, or until the onion is light golden, then pour in 250 ml (9 fl oz/1 cup) water. Return the lamb shanks to the dish.

Cook the shanks for 30 minutes, then pour the coconut milk into the dish and add the potatoes. Cover and cook over low heat for 1 hour, then add the green beans and cook for a further 15 minutes.

Just before serving, drizzle the lemon juice over the shanks and scatter with the coriander leaves.

SERVES 4

Vegetable and white bean soup

This is quite simply a big 'feel-good hug in a bowl' and perfect for a wintery Sunday night curled up in front of the television, watching your favourite movie. It's cram-packed with lots of healthy vegetables and the white beans, which are puréed, add a lovely silky-smooth texture. If you are vegetarian, then the pancetta can easily be dropped from the recipe.

2 tablespoons extra virgin olive oil
80 g (2³/4 oz) pancetta, finely chopped
2 brown onions, finely chopped
2 garlic cloves, crushed
1 teaspoon finely chopped sage
1 carrot, peeled and grated
1 parsnip, peeled and grated
1 celery stalk, thinly sliced
1 fresh bay leaf
1 litre (35 fl oz/4 cups) vegetable stock
400 g (14 oz/1 bunch) cavolo nero, trimmed and thinly sliced
2 zucchini (courgettes), diced
400 g (14 oz) tinned cannellini beans, drained and rinsed
70 g (2¹/2 oz/²/3 cup) finely grated parmesan cheese

Heat the olive oil in a large saucepan over medium heat. Add the pancetta and cook for 2–3 minutes, stirring to prevent the pancetta from catching on the bottom of the pan.

Add the onion, garlic and sage and cook for a further 3 minutes, or until the onion is light golden. Add the carrot, parsnip, celery and bay leaf. Stir for a few minutes to allow the vegetables to gently cook, then add the stock, cavolo nero and zucchini. Bring to the boil, then reduce the heat to low and simmer gently.

Meanwhile, put the cannellini beans in a food processor or blender and process to a purée. Add the purée to the soup and continue to cook for a further 5 minutes.

Ladle into four warmed soup bowls. Top with the parmesan and serve with warm bread.

SERVES 4

Chicken curry

Packed with great zesty flavours, this chicken curry is finished off with a simple paste of green chillies, coriander and mint, which gives it a wonderful fresh flavour, quite unlike most curries. It also freezes well, so make a double batch and keep half for a quick-fix midweek meal. Or, you can use it to fill a wintery Sunday night pie, topped with a puff pastry lid and sprinkled with sesame seeds.

1 kg (2 lb 4 oz) boneless, skinless chicken thigh fillets, cut into bite-sized pieces
3 onions, thinly sliced
35 g (1¼ oz/½ cup) shredded dried coconut
2 tablespoons tamarind purée
2 teaspoons finely grated fresh ginger
1 lemongrass stem, trimmed, bruised and cut into 4 cm (1½ inch) lengths
1 garlic clove, crushed
1 teaspoon ground turmeric
1 teaspoon red chilli powder
60 ml (2 fl oz/¼ cup) vegetable oil
30 g (1 oz/1 cup) coriander (cilantro) leaves
10 g (¼ oz/½ cup) mint leaves
4 green chillies, roughly chopped
2 tablespoons lemon juice
250 g (9 oz) plain yoghurt

Put the chicken in a wide heavy-based saucepan with the onion, coconut, tamarind, ginger, lemongrass, garlic, turmeric, chilli powder, oil and 500 ml (17 fl oz/2 cups) water. Bring to the boil, then reduce the heat to low. Cover and leave to simmer gently for 35 minutes, then remove the lid and increase the heat to high so the sauce boils down a little and starts to thicken.

Meanwhile, put the coriander, mint, chillies and lemon juice in a food processor or blender. Add 2 tablespoons water and process to form a smooth paste.

When the curry has reduced and the meat is thickly coated in the sauce, pour the fresh herb paste into the curry, stir to combine, then cook for a further 4 minutes.

Divide among four bowls and top with a spoonful of yoghurt. Serve with steamed rice and naan bread or soft flatbread.

SERVES 4

Chilli con carne

As we all know, travel isn't always glamorous. I recently found myself in a hotel room attempting to heat a piece of supermarket lasagne in a coffee cup. As I finally curled up with my cup of lasagne, I surprised myself with the thought that there really is something quite lovely about eating out of a cup. I know you are wondering where I'm going with this and the answer is that a friend of mine always serves chilli con carne at his parties in a cup, with a spoon, and it's become quite a favourite tradition.

2 tablespoons olive oil
1 onion, chopped
3 garlic cloves, crushed
2 large red chillies, seeded and chopped
1 teaspoon ground cumin
1 teaspoon ground coriander
1 teaspoon smoked paprika
1 teaspoon dried oregano
500 g (1 lb 2 oz) minced (ground) beef
250 ml (9 fl oz/1 cup) vegetable stock
400 g (14 oz) tinned diced tomatoes
2 tablespoons tomato paste (concentrated purée)
1 tablespoon soy sauce
1 cinnamon stick
400 g (14 oz) red kidney beans
1 red capsicum (pepper), about 300 g (10^1/$_2$ oz), diced
150 g (5^1/$_2$ oz) light sour cream
coriander (cilantro) sprigs, to serve

Heat the olive oil in a large heavy-based saucepan over medium heat, then add the onion, garlic, chilli, cumin, coriander, paprika and oregano. Cook for 5 minutes, or until the onion is soft and the spices are fragrant.

Add the beef and cook, stirring, for a further 5 minutes, or until well browned. Add the stock, tomatoes, tomato paste, soy sauce and cinnamon stick. Bring to the boil, then cover the pan, reduce the heat to low and simmer for 1 hour, stirring occasionally, until the meat is tender and the sauce has thickened.

Remove the lid and stir in the kidney beans and capsicum. Cover and cook for a further 20 minutes. Spoon into bowls and top with the sour cream and coriander sprigs.

SERVES 4

This is a meal that is always fun to eat, whether it's from a plate, bowl or out of a cup, with the night sky over your head.

weekend
platters

Gravlax with fennel and cucumber

It does take a bit of time to make this, so it's definitely one for a long weekend or a celebratory holiday, but it is so much fun to do and it's such a spectacular dish to serve that it's well worth that little bit of time spent forward planning.

The fennel salad cuts the richness of the salmon and the mustard–dill dressing adds a lovely herby sweetness to the mix.

500 g (1 lb 2 oz) rock salt
140 g (5 oz/²/3 cup) sugar
2 teaspoons coarsely crushed black peppercorns
60 g (2¹/4 oz/1 bunch) dill
900 g (2 lb) salmon fillet (one whole side), skin on and bones removed
rye crispbread, to serve

FENNEL SALAD
2 fennel bulbs (about 600 g/1 lb 5 oz)
2 Lebanese (short) cucumbers
1 teaspoon salt
2 tablespoons lemon juice
60 ml (2 fl oz/¹/4 cup) extra virgin olive oil
¹/2 teaspoon ground coriander

MUSTARD–DILL DRESSING
1 tablespoon dijon mustard
1 tablespoon caster (superfine) sugar
2 tablespoons apple cider vinegar
125 ml (4 fl oz/¹/2 cup) sunflower oil
2 tablespoons finely chopped dill (reserved from the bunch)

Put the rock salt in a bowl with the sugar and crushed peppercorns. Finely chop the dill and add it to the bowl, reserving 2 tablespoons for the dressing. Stir to combine. Line a shallow dish or tray with plastic wrap and put a little of the salt mixture over the base.

Place the salmon fillet, skin side down, on the bed of salt and then cover the fillet with the remaining salt mixture. Put another piece of plastic wrap over the fillet and then tightly wrap the plastic around the fish. Put a slightly smaller tray or cutting board on the fish and weigh it down with a heavy bowl or several tins. Refrigerate for 2 days, turning the fish every 12 hours.

To make the fennel salad, cut the fennel bulbs in half, reserving any fronds. Using a mandolin or very sharp knife, cut the fennel into paper-thin slices and place in a bowl. Thinly slice the cucumbers and add them to the fennel. Sprinkle with the salt and toss well to combine. Set aside for 30 minutes, then drain away any juices sitting in the base of the bowl. In a small bowl, combine the lemon juice, olive oil and coriander. Pour the dressing over the fennel and cucumber and toss to coat. Finely chop some of the fennel fronds and sprinkle them over the top.

To make the mustard–dill dressing, whisk the mustard, sugar and vinegar together, then whisk in the sunflower oil in a thin stream. Stir in the reserved dill and season with freshly ground black pepper.

Unwrap the fish and brush away any excess salt and herbs. Put the fillet onto a clean board and thinly slice with a very sharp knife. Cut the fillet as you would smoked salmon, starting at the tail end, holding the knife on the diagonal and cutting down towards the skin. Serve the sliced gravlax with the fennel salad, dressing and rye crispbread.

SERVES 8–10

weekend platters   *117*

Pulled pork with apple and fennel slaw

This is a fun party dish that's all about everyone diving in and helping themselves. Sure, you could make up little sliders for everyone, but I always think that to get a decent amount of pork and slaw on your bun you can't be tidy, delicate or restrained, and you really do need a supporting plate to catch the overflow!

It's also worth finding a supplier of good brioche buns, as they do add an elegant richness to this gutsy dish. However, any soft bun that isn't too doughy will work.

2 kg (4 lb 8 oz) boneless shoulder of pork, rind removed, excess fat trimmed
1 tablespoon sea salt
2 tablespoons light brown sugar
1 tablespoon smoked paprika
1 teaspoon fennel seeds
1 teaspoon chilli flakes
2 tablespoons olive oil
4 red onions, peeled and cut into wedges
2 red capsicums (peppers), cut into strips
2 garlic cloves, crushed
250 ml (9 fl oz/1 cup) apple juice or cider

APPLE AND FENNEL SLAW
2 lemons, juiced
3 green apples, such as granny smiths
2 fennel bulbs
1 handful flat-leaf (Italian) parsley leaves, finely chopped
60 ml (2 fl oz/¼ cup) extra virgin olive oil

soft brioche buns and mayonnaise, to serve

Preheat the oven to 150°C (300°F). Line a large roasting tin with a sheet of heavy-duty extra-wide foil.

Place the pork on a clean work surface. In a small bowl, combine the salt, brown sugar, paprika, fennel seeds and chilli flakes. Rub half of the salt mixture over the pork. Heat the olive oil in a large frying pan over high heat and sear the pork on all sides until just browned.

Meanwhile, put the onion, capsicum and garlic in the base of the prepared tin. Pour the apple juice over the vegetables. Add the seared pork to the tin and sprinkle with the remaining salt mixture. Cover the tin with another piece of foil and roast for 5 hours.

To make the apple and fennel slaw, put the lemon juice in a large bowl and season with sea salt and freshly ground black pepper. Peel and quarter the apples, then remove the cores and thinly slice with a mandolin or very sharp knife. As you slice the apple, add it into the lemon juice and toss to coat, to prevent the apple from browning. Trim and halve the fennel, then thinly slice it. Add the sliced fennel and chopped parsley to the apple. If there are any green fronds on the fennel, they can also be added to the slaw. Drizzle with the olive oil and toss to combine.

When the pork is cooked, pull the meat apart using two forks and mix it into the onion and capsicum mixture. Season to taste with sea salt and freshly ground black pepper. Serve the pork with the apple slaw, soft brioche buns and mayonnaise.

SERVES 8–10

Baked ricotta with caponata

I often make this when asked to 'bring a plate'. It's slightly unexpected and travels well, making it the perfect addition to the groaning table of salads and dips. The rich, salty–sweet flavours of the caponata are well suited to the milky simplicity of the ricotta, and the fresh oregano is a perfect accompaniment to anything with tomato. Spoon the caponata over just before serving, to keep the ricotta looking fresh.

If you don't have time to make the caponata, then the ricotta can be simply topped with fresh herbs, some olives or quartered and well-seasoned cherry tomatoes. However, the caponata is a great recipe in itself and is equally at home with grilled beef or lamb, seared tuna or spooned onto bruschetta.

500 g (1 lb 2 oz) fresh full-fat ricotta cheese
1/2 teaspoon finely chopped rosemary
35 g (1 1/4 oz/1/3 cup) finely grated parmesan cheese
1 egg, lightly beaten

CAPONATA
1 eggplant (aubergine), about 300 g (10 1/2 oz), cut into 2 cm (3/4 inch) cubes
80 ml (2 1/2 fl oz/1/3 cup) olive oil
1/2 red onion, thinly sliced
1 garlic clove, crushed
1 celery stalk, diced
2 ripe roma (plum) tomatoes, finely chopped
1 tablespoon sugar
1 tablespoon apple cider vinegar
6 sicilian green olives, pitted and finely chopped
1 tablespoon small salted capers, rinsed and drained
45 g (1 1/2 oz/1/3 cup) slivered almonds, toasted
oregano leaves, to serve

Preheat the oven to 180°C (350°F). Loosely line a 20 cm (8 inch) spring-form cake tin with a piece of baking paper. Sit the tin on a baking tray.

Put the ricotta in a large bowl with the rosemary, parmesan and egg. Stir to combine, then spoon the ricotta mixture into the prepared tin. Place the tray and tin in the oven and bake for 30–35 minutes, or until the ricotta is firm and lightly golden. Remove from the oven and set aside to cool to room temperature.

Meanwhile, to make the caponata, put the eggplant in a colander over a bowl. Sprinkle with salt and leave the eggplant to drain while you prepare the other ingredients.

Rinse the eggplant well to remove the salt, then drain and pat dry with paper towel. Heat half of the olive oil in a non-stick frying pan over medium heat. Add the eggplant and fry for 4–5 minutes, or until golden all over, then transfer to a plate.

Add the remaining oil to the pan and cook the onion and garlic until golden, then return the eggplant to the pan along with the celery, tomatoes and sugar. Cook for 5 minutes, then add the vinegar, olives, capers and almonds and cook for a further 1 minute.

Transfer the ricotta to a serving plate, spoon over the caponata and sprinkle with oregano leaves. Serve with crisp flatbread.

SERVES 8

Tomato tarte tatin with olive crème fraîche

The whole point of this tart is the caramelised texture of the base ingredients rubbing shoulders with the flaky buttery pastry, so please invest in a good-quality butter puff pastry.

You could also make versions of this tart using sweetly caramelised red onions or leeks, thinly sliced baby beetroot or thick rounds of zucchini. If you were going to try any of these options, I'd recommend replacing the tarragon with thyme.

2 tablespoons balsamic vinegar
2 tablespoons caster (superfine) sugar
1 teaspoon finely chopped tarragon
400 g (14 oz/1 punnet) heirloom tomatoes (tomato medley), halved
1 sheet good-quality frozen butter puff pastry, thawed
250 g (9 oz) crème fraîche
2 tablespoons finely chopped black olives
micro herbs, such as cress, to serve

Preheat the oven to 180°C (350°F). Generously grease a 20 cm (8 inch) ceramic pie dish with butter.

Put the vinegar, sugar and tarragon in the base of the pie dish, then add the tomatoes, cut side down. Bake in the oven for 30 minutes, then remove. Increase the oven temperature to 200°C (400°F).

Place the sheet of puff pastry over the tomatoes in the dish, tucking the edge of the pastry in around the tomatoes. Return the dish to the oven and bake for a further 25 minutes, or until the pastry is puffed up and golden brown.

Meanwhile, put the crème fraîche in a small serving bowl and stir in the chopped olives.

Remove the tart from the oven. Put a large serving plate over the pie dish and carefully flip it over. The tart should now be sitting on the plate with the tomatoes facing up. Scatter the cress over the tart and serve in slices, topped with a dollop of the crème fraîche.

SERVES 6

This is a beautiful way to use all those lovely, brightly coloured tomatoes that are now so readily available.

Pissaladière

A classic recipe from southern France, this tart celebrates the sour-sweet play-off that happens between the caramelised onions and the olive and anchovy topping. You can make this with a pizza dough or good-quality shop-bought puff pastry, but the pastry base I've included here is super simple. It uses olive oil rather than butter, so it can be quickly stirred together in a bowl. It feels a bit sneaky making it this way, but the end result is a surprisingly soft and flaky pastry.

TOPPING
80 ml (2½ fl oz/⅓ cup) extra virgin olive oil
900 g (2 lb) onions (about 6), peeled and thinly sliced
3 garlic cloves, crushed
1 teaspoon thyme leaves
½ teaspoon finely chopped rosemary
½ teaspoon sugar
1 teaspoon balsamic vinegar
2 tablespoons finely chopped flat-leaf (Italian) parsley, plus 1 small handful parsley leaves, to garnish
12 anchovies, halved lengthways
12 kalamata olives, pitted and halved lengthways

PASTRY
300 g (10½ oz/2 cups) plain (all-purpose) flour
1 teaspoon baking powder
½ teaspoon salt
125 ml (4 fl oz/½ cup) extra virgin olive oil
125 ml (4 fl oz/½ cup) chilled water

To make the topping, heat the olive oil in a wide heavy-based frying pan over low heat. Add the onion, cover the pan and cook for 20 minutes, or until the onion is lightly caramelised, stirring occasionally to prevent the onion catching on the base of the pan.

Add the garlic, thyme, rosemary, sugar and vinegar and cook for a further 15 minutes, or until the onion begins to melt and turns golden brown and is richly caramelised. Remove the pan from the heat, add the chopped parsley and stir to combine.

Preheat the oven to 200°C (400°F). Meanwhile, to make the pastry, put the flour, baking powder and salt in a large bowl. Stir to combine well. Put the olive oil and chilled water in a bowl and whisk to combine. Pour the liquid into the flour and mix with a wooden spoon for a few seconds until it comes together. If the dough is still quite wet, add a little flour and work it in with your hands.

Roll out the dough between two sheets of baking paper to form a 25 x 35 cm (10 x 14 inch) rectangle. Transfer the pastry and baking paper to a baking tray. Place a second tray on top of the paper-covered pastry and bake in the oven for 10 minutes. Remove the top tray and baking paper from the pastry and return to the oven for a further 10 minutes, or until the pastry is crisp and golden.

Spread the onion mixture over the pastry. Arrange the anchovies and olives over the top and return to the oven for a further 25 minutes. Sprinkle with the parsley leaves and serve with a mixed tomato salad or a green salad.

SERVES 6–8

Chicken liver parfait with a spiced cherry relish

Seductively rich in texture and flavour, this parfait is a great dish to make when friends are gathering for a few drinks. It can be made well ahead of time and served alongside crispy bread and sliced charcuterie meats. The cherry relish is not essential but it does add a lovely sweetness to the earthy tones of the parfait. It's a great addition to an elegant selection of pre-dinner nibbles, which will leave your guests feeling generously welcomed.

200 g (7 oz) unsalted butter
300 g (10¹/₂ oz) chicken livers, trimmed
2 fresh bay leaves, bruised
¹/₄ teaspoon ground allspice
2 garlic cloves, finely chopped
60 ml (2 fl oz/¹/₄ cup) brandy
2 tablespoons sour cream

SPICED CHERRY RELISH
300 g (10¹/₂ oz/1¹/₂ cups) bottled morello cherries, pitted and finely chopped
2 tablespoons balsamic vinegar
2 tablespoons brandy
2 tablespoons light brown sugar

Melt 50 g (1³/₄ oz) of the butter in a large non-stick frying pan over medium heat. When the butter starts to sizzle, add the chicken livers and bay leaves and cook for 1–2 minutes on each side, or until the livers are browned on the outside but are still pink in the middle. Remove the bay leaves and put the chicken livers and pan juices in a blender or food processor with a little sea salt and freshly ground black pepper.

Put another 50 g (1³/₄ oz) of butter into the pan and add the allspice and garlic. Cook over low heat for 1–2 minutes, or until the garlic is lightly golden but not burnt. Add the brandy and cook until most of the liquid has evaporated. Add the garlic and pan juices to the chicken livers in the blender and blend until the livers are puréed.

Cut the remaining butter into small dice and add it to the blender. Blend until well combined and smooth. Spoon the liver mixture into a serving bowl and stir through the sour cream. Smooth the top, then cover and refrigerate until ready to serve.

To make the spiced cherry relish, put the chopped cherries in a small saucepan with the vinegar, brandy and brown sugar. Simmer over low heat for about 5 minutes, or until the liquid has mostly evaporated and what remains is quite syrupy. Remove from the heat and spoon into a separate bowl.

Serve the chicken liver parfait with the spiced cherry relish and thinly sliced toasted sourdough bread.

SERVES 8

*Other suggestions for simple nibbles
to accompany the parfait are:*

SPICED NUTS

Preheat the oven to 170°C (325°F). Put 1 teaspoon each of cumin seeds, coriander seeds, mustard seeds and ground turmeric in a spice grinder or small blender and grind to a fine powder. Transfer the mixture to a large bowl and add 2 tablespoons light brown sugar, 1 tablespoon finely grated orange zest, 2 teaspoons sea salt and 100 g (3½ oz/about ⅔ cup) each of pecans, peanuts, cashews and macadamia nuts. Stir to combine, then add 2 tablespoons olive oil and mix well. Spread the nut mixture over a baking tray. Place the tray in the oven and bake, stirring occasionally, for 10–15 minutes, or until the nuts have coloured a little. Allow to cool completely before storing in an airtight container.

MARINATED OLIVES

Combine 500 g (1 lb 2 oz) mixed olives with 2 crushed garlic cloves, several thyme sprigs, 1 rosemary sprig, 1 bay leaf, some strips of lemon peel and 80 ml (2½ fl oz/⅓ cup) extra virgin olive oil. Cover and leave to marinate in the refrigerator overnight.

TAHINI DIP

Serve the tahini sauce on page 152 with crispbread and a selection of raw vegetables for dipping, such as baby carrots, cucumber wedges, trimmed green beans, thickly sliced fennel and trimmed radishes.

Whole baked salmon with ginger—tamarind dressing

Whole fish always look spectacular when served, and this is an easy way to cook the salmon without too much bother. However, remember to check your oven width before buying the fish.

The baked salmon can be served hot with steamed rice and Asian greens, or at room temperature with a selection of salads as part of a buffet for a larger gathering. Serve with accompaniments such as roast pumpkin wedges (page 176), green salad with buttermilk dressing (page 154) or the herb and lemon couscous (page 161).

2–3 kg (4 lb 8 oz–6 lb 12 oz) whole salmon
2 tablespoons olive oil
3 spring onions (scallions), sliced
4 limes
90 g (3¼ oz/1 bunch) coriander (cilantro), rinsed well
8 peppercorns
80 ml (2½ fl oz/⅓ cup) white wine
3 tablespoons tamarind purée
1 tablespoon grated palm sugar (jaggery) or light brown sugar
½ teaspoon ground cumin
2 large red chillies, seeded and thinly sliced
1 teaspoon soy sauce
1 heaped tablespoon finely grated fresh ginger
250 g (9 oz/1 bunch) watercress, rinsed and sprigs picked

Remove the salmon from the refrigerator 30 minutes before baking. Rinse under cold water and pat dry with paper towel. Preheat the oven to 180°C (350°F).

Cut two lengths of extra-wide heavy-duty foil slightly longer than the fish. Place one sheet of foil on a large baking tray and brush both pieces of foil with olive oil. Place the salmon on the foil-lined tray.

Fill the cavity of the fish with the sliced spring onions, 1 thinly sliced lime, 1 handful of the coriander leaves and the peppercorns. Cover the fish with the second sheet of foil, ensuring that the oiled surface sits over the fish. Bring the foil up around the fish carefully, crimping the edges of the foil together to seal it. Before the fish is completely sealed in the foil parcel, pour in the wine and then continue to seal.

Put the salmon in the oven and bake for 40 minutes. Turn the oven off and leave the fish in the closed oven for a further 45 minutes. During this time, do not open the foil.

Meanwhile, to make the ginger—tamarind dressing, put the tamarind purée in a bowl with 125 ml (4 fl oz/½ cup) water. Add the palm sugar, cumin, chilli, soy sauce, ginger and 1 tablespoon of finely chopped coriander stems. Stir to combine well.

Undo the foil and transfer the salmon to a platter. Peel away the skin from the top of the fish and spoon over the tamarind dressing. Cut the remaining limes into quarters. Arrange the lime quarters and the watercress sprigs around the fish and scatter with the remaining coriander leaves.

SERVES 8

Guinness baked ham with fig and ricotta salad

This is definitely a recipe for Christmas or a large gathering, as a baked ham is the easiest way to feed a crowd. It always looks spectacular and, when surrounded by a few simple salads, assorted relishes and mustards and crusty loaves, it oozes generosity. I've served it here with a fig and ricotta salad, one of my all-time favourites, but knowing how seasonal figs are, you could also serve it with the tomato and bocconcini salad (page 157), coleslaw (page 166), herb and lemon couscous (page 161), rocket and pear salad (page 156) or a combination of any of the above.

1 x 6 kg (13 lb) leg ham on the bone
125 ml (4 fl oz/1/2 cup) orange juice
500 ml (17 fl oz/2 cups) Guinness stout
3 star anise
185 g (6 1/2 oz/1 cup, lightly packed) light brown sugar
1 teaspoon ground ginger
1 teaspoon finely grated orange zest

FIG AND RICOTTA SALAD
135 g (4 3/4 oz/3 bunches) rocket (arugula), rinsed and stalks trimmed off
8 figs, quartered
500 g (1 lb 2 oz) fresh full-fat ricotta cheese
2 tablespoons caramelised balsamic vinegar
60 ml (2 fl oz/1/4 cup) extra virgin olive oil

Preheat the oven to 160°C (315°F). Using a small sharp knife, cut the skin around the thick end of the ham knuckle, without cutting into the flesh. You can do this in a line or a decorative zigzag. Ease the skin away from the fat by gently running your hand between the skin and the fat and gently lifting it away with your finger. Carefully peel back the skin in one whole piece, then turn the ham over and remove the rest of the skin.

Pour the orange juice and 375 ml (13 fl oz/1 1/2 cups) of the Guinness into a large roasting tin and add the star anise. Place the ham in the tin, fat side facing upwards. Cover the ham and roasting tin with extra-wide heavy-duty foil, completely sealing the ham. Put the ham in the oven and bake for 1 hour.

Meanwhile, to make a glaze, put the brown sugar, ginger, orange zest and remaining Guinness in a small bowl and stir to combine.

Remove the ham from the oven, remove the foil and carefully pour off the liquid in the tin. Using a sharp knife, score the fat in thinly spaced lines across the breadth of the ham. Spread half the glaze over the scored ham.

Increase the oven temperature to 200°C (400°F). Return the ham to the oven and bake, uncovered, for a further 30 minutes, basting with the remaining glaze every 10 minutes. Remove from the oven and transfer to a large serving platter.

Meanwhile, to make the fig and ricotta salad, put the rocket leaves on a separate platter and top with the figs and spoonfuls of the ricotta. Put the vinegar and olive oil in a small bowl, season with sea salt and freshly ground black pepper and whisk to combine. Drizzle the dressing over the salad just before serving.

SALAD SERVES 8, HAM SERVES MANY

Pork belly with lime pickle and green papaya salad

Like any recipe for pork belly, this is incredibly rich, so I've teamed the pork with a green papaya salad that is fresh-flavoured with a little chilli bite. If you're not excited by green papaya or find it difficult to source, serve the pork belly with roast pumpkin wedges (page 176) and a simple cos lettuce and cucumber salad.

4 green apples, such as granny smiths
250 ml (9 fl oz/1 cup) white wine
2 kg (4 lb 8 oz) piece boneless pork belly, rind removed
1 large garlic clove, peeled
1 teaspoon sea salt
1 tablespoon grated fresh ginger
2 tablespoons light brown sugar
3 tablespoons finely chopped Indian lime pickle
1 tablespoon freshly ground black pepper

GREEN PAPAYA SALAD
6 mint leaves
1^{1}/$_{2}$ tablespoons lime juice
1^{1}/$_{2}$ tablespoons fish sauce
1 tablespoon caster (superfine) sugar
1 small red chilli, seeded and finely chopped
500 g (1 lb 2 oz) green papaya
2 tablespoons finely chopped roasted peanuts
1 handful coriander (cilantro) leaves

Preheat the oven to 140°C (275°F). Line a deep roasting tin with extra-wide foil and then baking paper.

Peel, core and thickly slice the apples. Place the apple slices in the bottom of the prepared tin and pour the wine over them. Lay the pork belly on top of the apples.

Using the flat edge of a large knife, crush the garlic and then finely chop with the sea salt to form a paste. Combine the garlic paste, ginger, brown sugar and lime pickle in a small bowl.

Rub the paste over the pork and season with the pepper. Cover with foil and roast for 1 hour, then remove the foil and cook for a further 2 hours, or until tender.

Meanwhile, to make the green papaya salad, finely chop the mint leaves and put them in a large bowl with the lime juice, fish sauce, sugar and chilli. Stir until the sugar has dissolved, then set the dressing to one side. Peel the papaya and remove any seeds, then julienne the papaya with a mandolin. Add the papaya to the dressing, along with the peanuts and coriander leaves, and toss to combine.

Remove the pork from the oven and set it aside, loosely covered, for 15 minutes. Carve the pork into thick slices and serve with the apple slices and green papaya salad.

SERVES 6–8

Roast pork for summer or winter

Pork works so well with fruity flavours, and it's one of those roast meats that is great for either summer or winter dining. I've given you both options. The summer version is served with a colourful mango salad that features hot-pink pickled red onion and is, in its sunny brashness, the culinary equivalent of a Hawaiian shirt. The winter version is served with a gently spiced warm apple sauce, which sartorially could be linked to a well-loved and cosy jumper.

6-cutlet rack (1.6 kg/3 lb 8 oz) free-range pork, fat on
1 teaspoon fennel seeds
1/2 teaspoon dried Greek oregano
1 teaspoon sea salt
1/4 teaspoon ground white pepper
1 tablespoon apple cider vinegar
2 tablespoons olive oil

MANGO AND PICKLED ONION SALAD
1 large red onion, thinly sliced
1 tablespoon sea salt
1 teaspoon caster (superfine) sugar
2 tablespoons lemon juice
90 g (3 1/4 oz/2 bunches) rocket (arugula), rinsed and trimmed
2 mangoes, flesh removed and cut into wedges
60 ml (2 fl oz/1/4 cup) extra virgin olive oil

SPICED APPLE SAUCE
20 g (3/4 oz) butter
1 onion, finely chopped
2 garlic cloves, crushed
1/2 teaspoon Chinese five spice
5 green apples, such as granny smiths, peeled and finely chopped
60 ml (2 fl oz/1/4 cup) caramelised balsamic vinegar

Remove the pork from the fridge 30 minutes before roasting. Meanwhile, preheat the oven to 250°C (500°F). Using a sharp knife, score the pork skin by making parallel incisions on the surface, spacing the cuts about 5 mm (1/4 inch) apart.

Put the fennel seeds in a mortar and pestle or spice grinder and roughly grind. Add the oregano, sea salt and white pepper and stir to combine. Brush the apple cider vinegar over the scored skin, then rub the flavoured salt all over the pork rack.

Place the pork in a baking dish and drizzle with the olive oil. Roast for 15 minutes, then reduce the oven temperature to 170°C (325°F) and roast for a further 40 minutes. Remove from the oven, loosely cover and set aside to rest in the dish for 15 minutes.

To make the mango and pickled onion salad, put the sliced onion in a bowl and sprinkle with the sea salt. Stir to combine well, then set aside for 30 minutes. Rinse the salted onion under running water in a sieve, then squeeze to remove any excess water. Put the onion in a clean bowl and add the sugar and lemon juice. Set aside for a further 30 minutes, by which time you should have a bowl of neon-pink onions.

Put the rocket and mango wedges on a serving platter and scatter with the onion before drizzling with the olive oil. Season generously with freshly ground black pepper and a little sea salt.

To make the spiced apple sauce, put the butter, onion, garlic and five spice in a saucepan over medium heat. Cook for 2 minutes, or until the onion is just golden, then add the apple and 60 ml (2 fl oz/1/4 cup) water. Bring to the boil, then cover and simmer for about 15 minutes, or until the apple is soft and starting to fall apart. Stir through the balsamic vinegar. Serve warm.

Serve the roast pork with the rocket and mango salad or the spiced apple sauce. If you like, serve with the potato bake (page 168), crispy roast potatoes (page 170) or sweet potato wedges (page 176).

SERVES 6

Slow-cooked lamb shoulder

This is a warming, melt-in-the-mouth winter dish. The baby vegetables are cooked in the same dish as the lamb, so they absorb all the lovely rich flavours of rosemary, garlic and tomato. The parsley and lemon gremolata adds a final note of freshness and, if you love mint with your lamb, you could add a little finely chopped mint to the mix rather than the horseradish.

1.5 kg (3 lb 5 oz) boned shoulder of lamb
75 g (2½ oz/⅓ cup) semi-dried (sun-blushed) tomatoes, roughly chopped
30 g (1 oz/¼ cup) pitted black olives, roughly chopped
2 garlic cloves, thinly sliced
1 teaspoon rosemary leaves
60 ml (2 fl oz/¼ cup) olive oil
2 tablespoons tomato paste (concentrated purée)
250 ml (9 fl oz/1 cup) white wine
1 litre (35 fl oz/4 cups) vegetable stock
2 fresh bay leaves
12 small bulb spring onions, green stalks trimmed
600 g (1 lb 5 oz/2 bunches) dutch (baby) carrots, stalks trimmed and scrubbed
6 parsnips, peeled and halved lengthways

HORSERADISH GREMOLATA
15 g (½ oz/½ cup) finely chopped flat-leaf (Italian) parsley
1 tablespoon finely grated lemon zest
1 tablespoon finely grated fresh horseradish (optional)

Preheat the oven to 180°C (350°F). Cut a length of kitchen string into four 40 cm (16 inch) long pieces.

Lay the lamb, skin side down, on a clean surface. Scatter the tomatoes, olives, garlic and rosemary over the meat and then draw the sides together to make a semi-neat roll. Secure the roll with the pieces of string. Rub the lamb with the olive oil and season with sea salt and freshly ground black pepper.

Heat a large frying pan over high heat and brown the meat on all sides. Put the lamb in a large roasting tin. Stir the tomato paste and wine into the stock and pour it into the tin. Add the bay leaves. Cover and seal the tin with foil and place it in the oven. Cook for 3 hours, then remove the foil and add the spring onions, carrots and parsnips. Cover with the foil again and cook for a further 40 minutes.

While the lamb is cooking, make the horseradish gremolata. Combine the parsley, lemon zest and horseradish, if using, on a chopping board and chop once more to integrate the flavours.

Remove the lamb and vegetables from the oven and transfer to a warm serving platter. Sprinkle the gremolata over the lamb before serving.

SERVES 6

Duck breast with ginger and plums

There are a few foods in this world that I think are best left to the professionals, and roast duck is one of them. I know I shouldn't say things like that, but a roast duck is all about that amazing burnished and crisp skin, which I think can be hard to achieve in a home kitchen. This recipe is a quick-fix, kitchen-friendly option that uses only the breast fillet, which is, after all, the most succulent part of the duck. Its flavourings of white pepper, five spice, ginger and plums take their cue from those wonderful Chinatown ducks, but unites them all in what is basically a very simple roast.

6 boneless duck breast fillets, skin on
2 tablespoons light brown sugar
1 tablespoon sea salt
1/4 teaspoon ground white pepper
1/2 teaspoon Chinese five spice
125 ml (4 fl oz/1/2 cup) brandy
9 plums, halved and stones removed
4 cm (1 1/2 inch) piece fresh ginger, peeled and thinly sliced
1 large leek, white part only, rinsed and julienned
2 teaspoons olive oil
1 handful coriander (cilantro) leaves, to serve

Score the skin of the duck in a crisscross pattern. Put the brown sugar, sea salt, white pepper and five spice in a small bowl and stir to combine. Rub the flavoured salt into the duck skin.

Pour the brandy into a square storage container and add the duck breasts, skin side up. Cover and marinate in the refrigerator for a few hours or overnight.

Preheat the oven to 180°C (350°F). Put the plums, ginger and leek in a roasting dish, drizzle with the olive oil and season with sea salt and freshly ground black pepper. Roast in the oven for 20 minutes.

Meanwhile, heat a large non-stick frying pan over low–medium heat. Remove the duck breasts from the marinade, reserving the marinade. Put the duck breasts in the pan, skin side down, and cook for about 10 minutes. You want to slowly crispen the skin but not burn it, so keep an eye on the temperature of the pan.

Remove the plums from the oven and increase the oven temperature to 200°C (400°F). Put the duck breasts on top of the plums, skin side up. Pour over the reserved marinade and return the dish to the oven for a further 15 minutes.

Slice the duck breasts across the grain, spoon over the plums and leek and scatter with the coriander leaves. Serve with a side dish of steamed Asian greens and buttery brown rice.

SERVES 6

Peppered beef fillet with beetroot salad

I will state right now that this is a bit of an odd recipe, and I've encountered many a quizzical friend who has watched me cooking this and found themselves wondering aloud whether I knew what I was doing. Fortunately, there is a certain method to my madness.

The surface of the beef is covered in pepper and then left in the fridge to form a dry crust, which magically means it doesn't need to be seared, just cooked in a very hot oven. The timings are quite precise, so I always write them down on a post-it note and stick it next to the oven in case I start chatting to guests and lose the rhythm of what I'm doing. Rest assured, the beef is always perfectly cooked and early doubts are soon dismissed.

2 tablespoons freshly ground black pepper
900 g (2 lb) beef eye fillet, trimmed
600 g (1 lb 5 oz) beetroot (beets)
2 red capsicums (peppers), cut into 2 cm (3/4 inch) pieces
4 garlic cloves, peeled
4 rosemary sprigs
2 fresh bay leaves
80 ml (2½ fl oz/⅓ cup) extra virgin olive oil
2 tablespoons pomegranate molasses or balsamic vinegar
90 g (3¼ oz/2 bunches) rocket (arugula), rinsed and trimmed
horseradish cream, to serve

Rub the pepper over the beef. Put the beef on a tray and leave it in the refrigerator, uncovered, for at least one night but preferably two.

Preheat the oven to 200°C (400°F). Bring the beef to room temperature before cooking.

Lay a large sheet of heavy-duty foil on the work surface. Using rubber gloves, peel the beetroot and cut it into 2 cm (3/4 inch) cubes. Put the beetroot cubes on the foil along with the capsicum pieces, garlic cloves, rosemary sprigs and bay leaves. Season with sea salt and freshly ground black pepper and drizzle with a little of the olive oil. Wrap the beetroot up in the foil to form a sealed parcel, and place it on a baking tray. Cook for 40 minutes, then remove from the oven and set aside to cool.

Put the room-temperature beef fillet in a roasting tin and roast for 10 minutes, then turn the fillet over and roast for a further 5 minutes. Remove from the oven and season with sea salt, then cover with foil and rest for 15 minutes.

Unwrap the roasted beetroot and capsicum and transfer to a bowl. Add the pomegranate molasses and remaining olive oil and stir to combine. Arrange the rocket leaves on a platter and top with the dressed beetroot and capsicum.

Put the horseradish cream in a serving bowl. Drain any juices from the roasting tin and stir them into the horseradish cream.

Remove the foil and return the fillet to the oven for a further 15 minutes, then remove and cut into thick slices. Serve the beef with the beetroot and capsicum salad and the horseradish cream. If you like, serve with crispy roast potatoes (page 170) or the potato bake (page 168).

SERVES 6

Butterflied lamb with green sauce

The sauce I serve with this lamb is one of my favourites and I use it on many different dishes. Whenever I'm asked what ingredients I like to have close to hand, I always say fresh herbs and lemons, and that's what this sauce is all about. However, it's the preserved lemon that gives this lamb an extra zesty kick.

A jar of preserved lemons is another one of my store-cupboard essentials. Their intense spicy–salty, lemony flavour can rescue just about any dish that needs a bit of added excitement, from curries to couscous, steamed fish to barbecued chicken.

1 tablespoon olive oil
2 kg (4 lb 8 oz) butterflied leg of lamb
2 tablespoons sumac

GREEN SAUCE
20 g (³/4 oz/¹/2 cup) chopped coriander (cilantro) leaves
7 g (¹/4 oz/¹/4 cup) chopped flat-leaf (Italian) parsley
2 garlic cloves, crushed
2 tablespoons lemon juice
2 tablespoons chopped preserved lemon rind
1 teaspoon ground cumin
60 ml (2 fl oz/¹/4 cup) extra virgin olive oil

Preheat the oven to 200°C (400°F). Brush the olive oil over the skin and flesh of the lamb and then rub the sumac over the lamb. Season with a generous sprinkle of sea salt.

Heat a large frying pan over high heat until it is very hot. Sear the lamb on both sides for 3–4 minutes, or until browned. Transfer the lamb to a roasting dish and roast for 40–45 minutes.

To make the green sauce, put all the ingredients, except the olive oil, in a food processor and pulse to combine. With the motor running, slowly add the oil to form a thick paste.

Remove the lamb from the oven and transfer to a warm platter. Cover with foil and rest for 10 minutes. Thickly slice the lamb and serve with the green sauce. Serve with accompaniments such as the herb and lemon couscous (page 161) and a tomato salad.

SERVES 6

A good roast chook

A roast chicken is one of my all-time favourite meals. I make it when I feel flat and need cheering up and I make it when I'm happy and feel like celebrating. Basically, any excuse will do to fill the house with those wonderful roasty aromas, and to sit a golden-skinned bird on a platter surrounded with roast vegetables. If I have time, I make a stuffing infused with lovely herby flavours, but I'm just as happy with a chicken filled with garlic cloves and lemon quarters. I've given you a few stuffing options at the end of the recipe, to suit many inclinations.

LEMON AND HERB STUFFING
60 g (2¼ oz) butter
2 rindless bacon rashers (160 g/5½ oz), finely chopped
1 large onion, finely chopped
1 garlic clove, crushed
1 tablespoon finely chopped sage
1 celery stalk, finely diced
90 g (3¼ oz/1½ cups, lightly packed) fresh breadcrumbs
15 g (½ oz/1½ cup) finely chopped flat-leaf (Italian) parsley
1 tablespoon finely grated lemon zest
2 tablespoons lemon juice

TARRAGON BUTTER
60 g (2¼ oz) softened butter
1 tablespoon finely chopped tarragon
1 garlic clove, crushed

1 x 1.6 kg (3 lb 8 oz) whole chicken
500 ml (17 fl oz/2 cups) chicken stock
1–2 tablespoons extra virgin olive oil

To make the lemon and herb stuffing, melt the butter in a large frying pan over medium heat. Add the chopped bacon and cook for 2 minutes, then add the onion, garlic and sage and cook, stirring, for 3–4 minutes, or until the onion is soft. Add the celery and cook for a further 5 minutes. Transfer the onion and celery mixture to a large bowl and add the breadcrumbs, parsley, lemon zest and juice. Season with sea salt and freshly ground black pepper and stir to combine well.

To make the tarragon butter, put the softened butter in a bowl and stir in the chopped tarragon and garlic and season with sea salt and freshly ground black pepper.

Preheat the oven to 200°C (400°F). Rinse the chicken and then pat dry inside and out with paper towel. Run your fingers carefully between the skin and breast meat to make two large pockets. Fill each of these pockets with the tarragon butter. Fill the chicken cavity with the stuffing and secure the legs with kitchen string.

Transfer the chicken to a large roasting tin and add the stock. Brush the chicken with the olive oil and season generously with sea salt. Bake in the oven for 1½ hours. To test if the chicken is cooked, pull one of the legs away from the body—the juices that run out should be clear and not pink. If the chicken is still undercooked, return it to the oven for a further 10 minutes.

When the chicken is cooked, turn it over so it is lying breast side down. Cover with foil and rest for 15 minutes before serving.

SERVES 4–6

A few options:

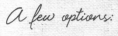 Instead of using tarragon to flavour the butter, use Indian lime pickle. Finely chop 2 tablespoons Indian lime pickle and add half to the butter and use the other half to rub over the chicken skin. Fill the cavity with whole garlic cloves, fresh coriander (cilantro) leaves and 1 quartered lime.

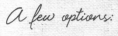 For a roast chicken with richer Italian flavours, replace the tarragon in the butter with some finely chopped prosciutto and add 110 g (3¾ oz/½ cup) finely chopped semi-dried (sun-blushed) tomatoes to the stuffing.

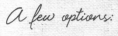 For a zesty lemon-flavoured chicken, rub the salty flesh of preserved lemon over the chicken before roasting. If you like, drizzle honey over the lemony chicken for the last 10 minutes of the roasting time.

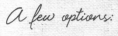 Fill the chicken cavity with a spiced couscous mixture and liberally sprinkle sumac over the oiled and seasoned skin.

Aromatic butterflied chicken

For this recipe, I've given instructions for cooking the chicken in the oven, but you could just as easily cook it in a covered barbecue over a low to medium heat.

This is a really delicious way to cook chicken and if I have friends over I usually double the recipe and cook two chickens. If you are time poor, you can make the paste and prepare the chicken the day before.

PASTE
90 g (3¹/4 oz/1 bunch) coriander (cilantro)
1 lemongrass stem, white part only, thinly sliced
45 g (1¹/2 oz/¹/3 cup) coarsely chopped macadamia nuts
¹/4 red onion, coarsely chopped
2 cm (³/4 inch) piece fresh ginger, coarsely chopped
2 long green chillies, coarsely chopped
4 kaffir lime leaves, thinly sliced
2 tablespoons extra virgin olive oil
1 tablespoon grated palm sugar (jaggery) or light brown sugar
1 teaspoon sesame oil
¹/2 teaspoon sea salt
¹/2 teaspoon ground white pepper

1 x 1.6 kg (3 lb 8 oz) whole chicken
1 lime, quartered

To make the paste, first rinse the bunch of coriander and then roughly chop the roots and stems, reserving the leaves for serving. Put the roots and stems in a food processor with the remaining paste ingredients and whiz until they have formed a thick paste.

Line a baking tray with baking paper. To butterfly the chicken, use a sharp knife or kitchen scissors to cut the chicken on both sides of the backbone; remove the backbone. Open the chicken out, turn it over and then flatten it by pressing down along the breastbone with the heel of your hand. Place the chicken on the prepared tray and rub the aromatic paste over the skin and flesh. Leave the chicken to marinate for 30 minutes.

Preheat the oven to 200°C (400°F). Roast the chicken for 50 minutes, or until the chicken is cooked through. To test if the chicken is cooked, pull one of the legs away from the body—the juices that run out should be clear and not pink. Remove from the oven and squeeze some lime juice over the chicken. Cover the chicken with foil and rest for 5 minutes.

Cut the chicken into pieces and arrange on a platter with the remaining lime quarters. Scatter the coriander leaves over the top. Serve with steamed Asian greens and rice.

SERVES 4–6

Seafood paella

Paella is a great dinner party meal and if you are going to cook it often, then it's worth investing in a proper paella pan, good-quality paprika (look for brightly coloured tins of paprika, not the generic herb jars) and a nice bottle of Spanish sherry. This recipe serves six but the quantity can easily be changed to suit the number of guests and is only constrained by the size of your pan.

You can also use this recipe as a base for a vegetarian paella, substituting the chicken and prawns with eggplant, doubling the capsicum, replacing the chicken stock with vegetable stock, and perching artichoke halves in the rice instead of mussels.

1 kg (2 lb 4 oz) mussels
1 teaspoon smoked paprika
1 teaspoon sweet paprika
1/2 teaspoon chilli powder
a generous pinch of saffron threads
100 ml (3 1/2 fl oz) olive oil
2 boneless, skinless chicken thigh fillets, cut into 2 cm (3/4 inch) pieces
12 raw prawns (shrimp), peeled and deveined, tails left intact

3 green chillies, seeded and chopped
6 garlic cloves, chopped
2 red onions, chopped
1 red capsicum (pepper), diced
350 g (12 oz) calasparra rice
125 ml (4 fl oz/1/2 cup) fino sherry
1.5 litres (52 fl oz/6 cups) chicken stock
1 handful coriander (cilantro) leaves
2 lemons, cut into wedges

Clean the mussels under cold running water, scrubbing them to remove any barnacles or bits of hairy beard. Discard any broken mussels or open ones that don't close when tapped on the kitchen bench. Rinse well.

Put the smoked and sweet paprikas and chilli powder in a small bowl and stir to combine. Put the saffron threads in a separate small bowl and cover with 2–3 tablespoons of boiling water.

Heat half of the olive oil in a large paella pan or large, deep frying pan over high heat and add half the paprika and chilli mixture. Stir the spices into the oil, then add the chicken and cook for 4 minutes. Add the prawns and cook for 1–2 minutes on each side, or until coloured and beginning to curl. Remove the chicken and prawns to a bowl.

Heat the remaining oil in the pan over medium heat and add the remaining paprika mixture, the green chilli, garlic and onion and cook for 2 minutes, or until the onion is soft. Add the capsicum and stir for 1 minute before adding the rice. Stir for 2 minutes to coat the rice in the spices, then add the sherry and the saffron water and threads. Cook for 2 minutes, or until the liquid has been absorbed, then add the stock.

Increase the heat to medium–high and cook the rice for 10–15 minutes, or until the stock is mostly absorbed. Return the chicken and prawns to the pan and add the mussels.

Cover the pan with foil or a fitted lid and cook for 1–2 minutes, or until all the mussels have opened. Remove from the heat and sprinkle with coriander leaves. Serve with the lemon wedges.

SERVES 6

on the side

Eggplant salad
with tahini sauce

This salad celebrates the silky fleshiness of the eggplant. The flavours are earthy and robust and it's a salad that would work well with either lamb, beef or seared tuna.

The tahini sauce is one of my favourites and when I'm not serving it drizzled over this eggplant salad, I'll whip it up as a dip for crudités and crackers.

6 long green chillies
2 eggplants (aubergines) (600 g/1 lb 5 oz in total)
3 large ripe tomatoes
60 ml (2 fl oz/¼ cup) extra virgin olive oil
1 garlic clove, peeled
½ teaspoon sea salt
1 teaspoon ground cumin
15 g (½ oz/½ cup) coriander (cilantro) leaves, plus extra to garnish

TAHINI SAUCE
135 g (4¾ oz/½ cup) tahini
1 tablespoon lemon juice
sea salt and ground white pepper

Heat the grill (broiler) or barbecue plate to medium. Cut the chillies in half lengthways and use a teaspoon to scrape away the seeds. Pierce the eggplants and tomatoes with a skewer a few times and rub some of the olive oil over their skins.

Put the chillies, eggplants and tomatoes on a baking tray and place under the hot grill or on the barbecue plate. Grill, turning occasionally, until the vegetables are blackened all over. Transfer to a bowl, cover with plastic wrap and set aside until cool.

Using the flat edge of a large knife, crush the garlic clove and then finely chop it with the sea salt to form a paste. Work the cumin into the paste and then add the coriander leaves and finely chop. Put the green paste in a large bowl with the remaining olive oil and stir to combine.

To make the tahini sauce, put the tahini in a bowl and add the lemon juice. Stir several times, then add 80 ml (2½ fl oz/⅓ cup) water and continue to stir until smooth. Season to taste with sea salt and ground white pepper.

Remove most of the blackened skin from the vegetables. Roughly chop them and add to the bowl with the green paste. Stir to combine and then transfer to a serving bowl or plate. Drizzle the tahini sauce over the eggplant salad and garnish with the extra coriander leaves.

SERVES 4–6

Green salad with buttermilk dressing

Mint, dill, parsley, chive, fennel and chervil ... this chunky herby salad with its delicate milky dressing is a pure celebration of spring and, as such, its flavours are intensely green. Serve it with seared or roast lamb, pan-fried veal or spicy barbecued chicken.

BUTTERMILK DRESSING
2 tablespoons apple cider vinegar
1 tablespoon lemon juice
1 garlic clove, finely chopped
2 anchovies, finely chopped
1/4 teaspoon caster (superfine) sugar
125 ml (4 fl oz/1/2 cup) extra virgin olive oil
125 ml (4 fl oz/1/2 cup) buttermilk
1 tablespoon finely chopped mint
1 tablespoon finely chopped dill

100 g (31/2 oz) sugarsnap peas, trimmed and halved
310 g (11 oz/2 bunches) asparagus, trimmed and halved lengthways
3 zucchini (courgettes), cut into long wedges
150 g (51/2 oz/1 bunch) broccolini, trimmed and halved lengthways
2 Lebanese (short) cucumbers, cut into chunks
1 fennel bulb, thinly sliced, green fronds reserved and finely chopped
1 handful flat-leaf (Italian) parsley leaves
20 g (3/4 oz/1 bunch) chives, trimmed and cut into 2 cm (3/4 inch) lengths
1 handful chervil

To make the buttermilk dressing, combine all the ingredients in a screw-top jar and shake to combine.

Bring a large saucepan of salted water to the boil and blanch the sugarsnap peas, asparagus, zucchini and broccolini for 2–3 minutes, or until they turn emerald green. Drain and rinse under cold water, then transfer to a large bowl. Add the cucumber and fennel and toss gently to combine.

Arrange the green vegetables on a serving plate, spoon over the buttermilk dressing and scatter with the parsley, chives, chervil and chopped fennel fronds.

SERVES 6–8

Rocket and pear salad

Rocket and pear salad is one of those classic dishes that goes with just about anything and which I could also happily eat by the bowlful for lunch. Most of the ingredients are interchangeable, as it's really all about the combination of sweet fruit with creamy cheese, bitter leaves and crunchy nuts. You could replace the pear with apple, swap the almonds for walnuts, and exchange the parmesan for crumbled goat's cheese—any of these variations would be equally delicious.

160 g (5½ oz/1 cup) whole almonds
2 tablespoons lemon juice
2 beurre bosc pears
200 g (7 oz) rocket (arugula) leaves, trimmed
70 g (2½ oz) parmesan cheese, shaved
80 ml (2½ fl oz/⅓ cup) extra virgin olive oil

Preheat the oven to 180°C (350°F). Put the almonds on a baking tray and roast in the oven for 10 minutes, then remove and set aside to cool.

Put the lemon juice in a large bowl and season with sea salt and freshly ground black pepper. Quarter the pears and remove the cores, then thinly slice them. As you slice the pears, add them to the lemon juice and toss several times to coat well. The lemon juice will prevent the pears from browning.

Roughly chop the almonds. Arrange the rocket leaves on a serving plate and add the sliced pears, parmesan and almonds. Add the olive oil to the remaining lemon juice in the bowl, whisk to combine and then pour the dressing over the salad.

SERVES 6

Heirloom tomato and bocconcini salad

I almost didn't include this salad because it barely rates as a recipe; however, we sometimes need to be reminded of the obvious and I honestly don't think you can beat a simply prepared salad of beautifully ripe summer tomatoes. I will add that the tomatoes should be at room temperature and it's important to let the seasoned tomatoes sit for a little while to allow the salt to draw out some of the lovely tomato juices. It's also important to use a wonderfully aromatic olive oil.

Simple dishes like this depend on the quality of the ingredients used; underripe tomatoes straight from the fridge and stale oil will not create culinary wonders.

800 g (1 lb 12 oz/2 punnets) mixed heirloom tomatoes (tomato medley)
½ red onion, thinly sliced
3 green chillies, seeded and finely chopped
1 tablespoon red wine vinegar
60 ml (2 fl oz/¼ cup) extra virgin olive oil
1 garlic clove, crushed
1 handful basil leaves
250 g (9 oz) bocconcini (fresh baby mozzarella cheese)

Depending on their size, cut the tomatoes into halves or quarters. Arrange the tomatoes on a serving platter and scatter the onion and chilli over the top. Season generously with sea salt and freshly ground black pepper. Set aside for 30 minutes, to allow the flavours to develop.

Meanwhile, put the vinegar, olive oil and garlic in a small screw-top jar and shake to blend. Pour the dressing over the tomatoes and then top with the basil leaves and bocconcini.

SERVES 4–6

Salad of crispy carrots and herby freekah

Anyone who knows me well would think that the only reason this salad is in this book is so I can say 'crispy carrots and herby freekah'. It's not the case, although I did have lots of fun saying it over and over again.

The carrots in this recipe are cut into thin ribbons, flavoured with cumin and roasted until crispy, then used to decorate the top of an earthy and extremely healthy plate of kale and freekah. It's as much fun to eat as it is to say!

175 g (6 oz/1 cup) wholegrain freekah
1/2 teaspoon sea salt
4 carrots
1 tablespoon olive oil
1 teaspoon ground cumin
2 celery stalks, thinly sliced
7 g (1/4 oz/1/4 cup) chopped flat-leaf (Italian) parsley
1 tablespoon finely chopped mint
2 tablespoons lemon juice
1 tablespoon finely chopped preserved lemon rind
180 g (61/2 oz/2 cups) thinly sliced curly kale leaves
60 ml (2 fl oz/1/4 cup) extra virgin olive oil

Preheat the oven to 180°C (350°F). Line a baking tray with baking paper.

Put the freekah in a saucepan with 1.5 litres (52 fl oz/6 cups) water. Add the sea salt and bring to the boil. Reduce the heat to low and cook for 45 minutes.

Meanwhile, peel the carrots and then use the vegetable peeler to remove ribbons of carrot. Put the olive oil and cumin in a bowl and season with sea salt and freshly ground black pepper. Add the carrot ribbons and gently toss to evenly coat in the oil. Transfer the carrot ribbons to the prepared tray and arrange them evenly over the tray. Place in the oven and bake for 30 minutes, turning occasionally, or until the carrots are a little crispy. Remove from the oven.

When the freekah is cooked, drain well and transfer to a large bowl. Add the celery, parsley, mint, lemon juice and preserved lemon and stir to combine.

Put the kale in a separate bowl and add the olive oil. Using your hands, work the oil into the kale. This will help to soften the kale and make it a little less springy. Add the kale to the other ingredients and stir to combine. Season to taste with sea salt and freshly ground black pepper.

Arrange the freekah salad on a serving plate and top with the crispy carrot ribbons.

SERVES 4–6

Ruby grapefruit, fennel and black olive salad

I love ruby grapefruit and I love shaved fennel, so it's not a surprise that this is one of my favourite salads. It can be eaten by itself as a refreshing summer entrée or lunchtime salad, or can be served alongside grilled fish or seared prawns.

Try to find a fennel bulb that still has its green fronds attached. Finely chop the fronds and add them to the salad for a lovely intense aniseed flavour and a lively burst of fresh colour.

2 ruby grapefruits
1 fennel bulb, thinly sliced, green fronds reserved and finely chopped
80 g (2³/₄ oz/¹/₂ cup) small ligurian olives
2 celery stalks, thinly sliced
1 teaspoon lemon juice
60 ml (2 fl oz/¹/₄ cup) extra virgin olive oil
1 handful flat-leaf (Italian) parsley leaves

Slice away the skin of the grapefruits, ensuring that you remove all the white pith as you do this. Holding the grapefruit over a large bowl to catch the juices, cut away the grapefruit segments by running your knife alongside the membranes. Add the segments to the bowl. Squeeze any remaining juice from the membranes before discarding them.

Add the fennel to the bowl along with the olives, celery, lemon juice, olive oil and parsley. Toss gently to combine, then arrange on a serving platter. Sprinkle with the chopped fennel fronds.

SERVES 4

Herb and lemon couscous

This is my easy go-to salad whether I'm feeding myself or a crowd. It's filling, has lots of punchy flavours and can easily be adjusted to any number of people and any range of ingredients. To this basic recipe, you could also add some toasted pine nuts, finely chopped preserved lemon rind, toasted flaked almonds, thinly sliced dried apricots, coarsely chopped pistachio nuts or finely chopped semi-dried tomatoes.

190 g (6¾ oz/1 cup) instant couscous
20 g (¾ oz) butter
250 ml (9 fl oz/1 cup) boiling water
finely grated zest and juice of 1 lemon
7 g (¼ oz/¼ cup) finely chopped flat-leaf (Italian) parsley
10 g (¼ oz/¼ cup) finely chopped coriander (cilantro) leaves
1 handful mint leaves, thinly sliced
2 Lebanese (short) cucumbers, finely diced
60 ml (2 fl oz/¼ cup) extra virgin olive oil

Put the couscous in a large bowl with the butter. Season with a little sea salt and freshly ground black pepper and then pour in the boiling water. Stir to combine, cover with plastic wrap and sit for 5 minutes to allow the water to absorb, then use a fork to fluff up the grains. Cover again and set aside for a further 5 minutes. Rub the grains with your finger tips to remove any lumps.

Add the lemon zest, herbs and cucumber and stir to combine before transferring to a serving bowl. Whisk the olive oil and lemon juice together to make a dressing. Drizzle the dressing over the couscous.

SERVES 4–6

Almond and cauliflower 'couscous'

Not only is this salad delicious but it's healthy as well. Once you've made it a few times, you can start to build on the basic recipe by playing around with some added flavours— grated beetroot, diced roast pumpkin, watercress, feta, goat's cheese and quinoa would all work well. The possibilities are endless, so it's a good idea to write down what you used in your favourite version so you don't forget.

2 garlic cloves, finely chopped
1 teaspoon ground cumin
1/2 teaspoon ground coriander
2 tablespoons extra virgin olive oil, plus extra to serve
2 red onions, thinly sliced
3 tomatoes, diced
80 g (2 3/4 oz/1/2 cup) whole almonds
1 tablespoon light soy sauce
250 g (9 oz) cauliflower
2 handfuls flat-leaf (Italian) parsley leaves, roughly chopped
2 tablespoons lemon juice

Preheat the oven to 180°C (350°F). Line two baking trays with baking paper (you will need a large tray for the vegetables).

In a large bowl, combine the garlic, cumin, coriander and olive oil. Stir to combine, then add the onion and tomato. Toss to combine, then arrange the onion and tomato on the large tray. Season with a little sea salt and freshly ground black pepper. Roast in the oven for 1 hour, stirring occasionally to ensure that the onion browns evenly.

Put the almonds on the second tray and drizzle with the soy sauce. Toss to coat the almonds in the soy sauce. Cook in the oven for 10 minutes, then remove and set aside to cool.

Finely chop the cauliflower. This can be done in a large food processor or by hand with a sharp knife. The cauliflower should look like fine crumbs. Put the cauliflower in a large bowl with the parsley and lemon juice.

Coarsely chop the almonds and add them to the bowl along with the cooked onion and tomato. Toss to combine and serve drizzled with a little olive oil.

SERVES 4–6

Confit tomatoes

These are two of my favourite tomato condiments. Whenever I have a few too many ripe tomatoes in my kitchen bowl, I make up a tray of confit tomatoes. Once stored in the fridge under oil they will keep for about 2 weeks, and I like to add them to salads, sandwiches, chicken stuffing or pasta sauces.

On the other hand, the tomato and chilli relish is something I plan to make, often around Christmas time so I can give jars of the relish as festive gifts. It's fantastic served with sausages, roast vegetables and just about everything in between.

8 ripe roma (plum) tomatoes
4 garlic cloves
6 thyme sprigs
80 ml (2¹/2 fl oz/¹/3 cup) extra virgin olive oil
8 basil leaves (optional)

Preheat the oven to 140°C (275°F). Line a baking tray with baking paper.

Cut the tomatoes into quarters lengthways. If the tomatoes are large, you may need to cut them again to make smaller wedges. Put the tomatoes on the prepared tray, cut side up, and sprinkle generously with sea salt and freshly ground black pepper.

Bruise the garlic cloves with the side of a large knife. Add them to the tray, then scatter the thyme sprigs over the top. Roast the tomatoes in the oven for 2 hours, or until they are wrinkled and slightly blackened.

Remove from the oven and set aside to cool. Transfer the tomatoes and garlic to a storage container (or sterilised jars) and pour over the olive oil. If you like, add some torn basil leaves. Store in the refrigerator for up to 2 weeks.

Tomato and chilli relish

10 large red chillies
80 ml (2¹/2 fl oz/¹/3 cup) olive oil
1 teaspoon cumin seeds
1 teaspoon mustard seeds
1 teaspoon ground turmeric
2 teaspoons finely grated fresh ginger
4 garlic cloves, finely chopped
1 kg (2 lb 4 oz) ripe tomatoes, roughly chopped
110 g (3³/4 oz/¹/2 cup) caster (superfine) sugar
125 ml (4 fl oz/¹/2 cup) apple cider vinegar
1 tablespoon fish sauce

Slice the chillies in half lengthways, remove most of the seeds and then thinly slice.

Heat the olive oil in a heavy-based saucepan over medium heat and add the cumin seeds, mustard seeds, turmeric and ginger. When the mustard seeds begin to pop, add the garlic and chilli. Stir a few times, then add the chopped tomatoes, sugar and vinegar.

Bring to the boil, then reduce the heat to low and simmer, stirring occasionally, for 2 hours, or until the relish has thickened. Add the fish sauce and stir to combine.

Spoon the relish into a sterilised 500 ml (17 fl oz/2 cup) jar. Seal with the lid, allow to cool and then refrigerate. Store in the refrigerator for up to 4 weeks.

Corn and red capsicum salad

Brightly coloured and richly flavoured, this salad works well with spicy barbecued chicken, sticky pork ribs (page 74) and grilled steak. Add some re-fried beans and sour cream and you also have a great vegetarian filling for tortillas and tacos.

2 tablespoons extra virgin olive oil
2 red onions, sliced
1 garlic clove, crushed
1 tablespoon ground cumin
1 teaspoon thyme leaves
3 corn cobs
2 red capsicums (peppers), diced
7 g (1/4 oz/1/4 cup) coarsely chopped mint leaves
20 g (3/4 oz/1/2 cup) coarsely chopped coriander (cilantro) leaves
1 tablespoon pomegranate molasses
1/2 teaspoon Tabasco sauce

Heat the olive oil in a large non-stick frying pan over medium heat and add the onion, garlic, cumin and thyme. Cook for 10 minutes, or until the onion is starting to caramelise.

Meanwhile, remove the corn kernels from the cobs by running a sharp knife down the side of the cobs. Add the capsicum and corn kernels to the onion and cook for a further 10 minutes, or until the corn is golden.

Remove from the heat and transfer to a serving bowl. Add the chopped mint and coriander, the pomegranate molasses and Tabasco sauce. Stir to combine and then season to taste before serving.

SERVES 4–6

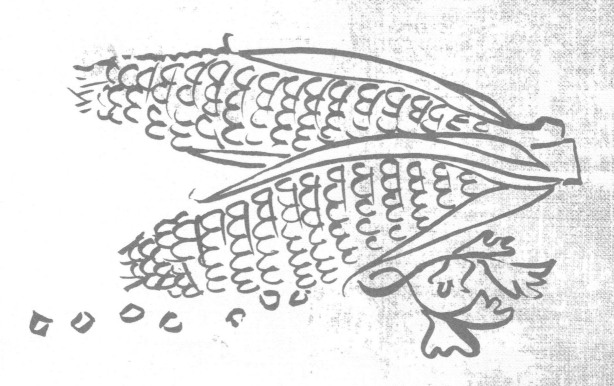

Coleslaw with lemon–mustard mayonnaise

Learning to make real mayonnaise is one of those things you just have to do, for two reasons. Firstly, home-made mayonnaise tastes so much better than the shop-bought version and given it only uses natural ingredients, it's better for you as well. Secondly, only by making mayonnaise will you realise how much oil is actually in it and you will then forever show restraint. I only make this point because salads should only ever be lightly coated in mayonnaise and this coleslaw is no exception.

LEMON–MUSTARD MAYONNAISE
2 egg yolks
1 tablespoon dijon mustard
1 tablespoon lemon juice
80 ml (2½ fl oz/⅓ cup) neutral oil, such as grapeseed oil
80 ml (2½ fl oz/⅓ cup) olive oil
1 teaspoon finely grated lemon zest

COLESLAW
225 g (8 oz/3 cups) thinly sliced Chinese cabbage (wong bok)
225 g (8 oz/3 cups) thinly sliced red cabbage
3 spring onions (scallions), thinly sliced
1 red capsicum (pepper), finely diced
50 g (1¾ oz/½ cup) flaked almonds, toasted
20 g (¾ oz/½ cup) coarsely chopped curly parsley

To make the lemon–mustard mayonnaise, put the egg yolks in a bowl and add the mustard and lemon juice. Slowly add the neutral oil, drop by drop, whisking continuously with a hand-held whisk to form a smooth paste. When all the neutral oil has been added, slowly add the olive oil in a thin stream while continuing to whisk.

Stir in the lemon zest and season to taste with sea salt and freshly ground black pepper. Transfer to a 250 ml (9 fl oz/1 cup) screw-top jar and refrigerate until ready to use.

To make the coleslaw, combine all the ingredients in a large bowl. Add just enough mayonnaise to lightly coat all the ingredients.

SERVES 4–6

Buttery potato bake

A potato bake is a great way to prepare potatoes in advance and is perfect for those wanting a change from the usual mashed potatoes. The bake can be kept in the pan it was cooked in and then reheated in the oven whenever you're ready to serve it, or if you're cooking a no-fuss dinner like grilled steaks, you can make it fresh.

I like to use dutch cream potatoes for this recipe as their waxy, buttery-yellow flesh holds up well when cooked, but any waxy or all-round potato, such as nicola or desiree, would work just as well.

80 g (2³/4 oz) butter
1 teaspoon finely chopped rosemary
1 teaspoon finely chopped sage, plus 8 whole leaves, extra
1 garlic clove, finely chopped
1 teaspoon sea salt
1/4 teaspoon ground white pepper
1.2 kg (2 lb 12 oz) waxy potatoes, such as dutch creams, or all-purpose potatoes, such as desiree

---

Preheat the oven to 180°C (350°F). Put the butter in a small saucepan over low heat and add the chopped rosemary, sage, garlic, sea salt and white pepper. When the butter has melted, remove from the heat.

Line an ovenproof frying pan or a 20 cm (8 inch) pie tin with baking paper. Brush with some of the flavoured butter and then arrange the whole sage leaves in a decorative flower pattern on the base of the pan.

Peel the potatoes and slice them very thinly. A mandolin is perfect for this task, but if you don't have one use a very sharp knife. Place a layer of potato slices in the pan, starting in the centre and fanning the pieces out over the base to form a petal pattern. Brush with some of the butter and then cover with another layer of potato slices. Repeat the process until all the potatoes have been used. Brush the remaining butter over the last layer of potato.

Bake for 1 hour, or until the potatoes are crispy and golden. Turn out onto a warm plate and serve in thick wedges.

SERVES 6

The crispiest roast potatoes

Roast potatoes need no introduction except to say that the potato monster inside me would probably double the recipe in the hope that there would be cold leftovers.

The roast new potatoes are a simpler approach and are as much about the added flavours as they are about the potatoes, so feel free to add spices and diced pumpkin to the potatoes, or sliced zucchini, garlic and lemon thyme.

1 kg (2 lb 4 oz) floury potatoes, such as king edward, peeled and quartered
2 tablespoons extra virgin olive oil
40 g (1½ oz) butter
1 teaspoon rosemary leaves

Preheat the oven to 200°C (400°F). Put the potatoes in a large saucepan and cover with cold water. Bring to the boil and cook for 5 minutes. Drain in a colander and leave to steam-dry for a few minutes. Toss the potatoes around in the colander to roughen up the surface.

Put the olive oil, butter and rosemary in a large roasting tin and sprinkle with a generous amount of sea salt and freshly ground black pepper. Put the tin in the hot oven for 5 minutes to heat.

Add the potatoes to the hot tin and roast for 1 hour, turning the potatoes every 20 minutes, until golden and crispy.

SERVES 4

Roast new potatoes

1 kg (2 lb 4 oz) new potatoes, washed
60 ml (2 fl oz/¼ cup) olive oil
1 lemon, juiced
6 rosemary sprigs
6 garlic cloves, bruised
12 green olives
250 g (9 oz/1 punnet) cherry tomatoes

Preheat the oven to 180°C (350°F). Put the potatoes in a large saucepan and cover with cold water. Bring to the boil, then cover the pan with a lid and remove from the heat. Sit, covered, for 15 minutes, then drain.

Put the boiled potatoes in a large roasting tin. Using the back of a large spoon, lightly crush each potato until it just begins to split. Drizzle the potatoes with the olive oil and lemon juice, then add the rosemary sprigs, garlic cloves, olives and tomatoes. Season generously with sea salt.

Roast in the oven for 40 minutes, or until the potatoes are crisp and golden brown.

SERVES 4

Smashed potato and kale with anchovy—herb sauce

This is a comforting combination of buttery potatoes and good-for-you greens, with a little bit of garlic thrown in for good measure. It's a great side dish for sausages, grilled chops and roast beef. Or, if you like potatoes as much as I do, it's a cosy midweek dinner as is—and even better with the addition of a little crispy bacon.

I've added the herb sauce in case you want to get a little bit fancy, but it really doesn't need it—you could simply serve the potato drizzled with a little extra virgin olive oil.

ANCHOVY—HERB SAUCE
1 handful flat-leaf (Italian) parsley leaves, finely chopped
10 mint leaves, finely chopped
1 garlic clove, finely chopped
3 anchovy fillets, finely chopped
1 tablespoon small salted capers, rinsed
1 teaspoon dijon mustard
1 tablespoon lemon juice
80 ml (2^{1}/2 fl oz/^{1}/3 cup) extra virgin olive oil

SMASHED POTATO
800 g (1 lb 12 oz) waxy potatoes, such as dutch creams, peeled
400 g (14 oz/1 bunch) curly kale or cavolo nero, leaves trimmed from stalks and rinsed
80 g (2^{3}/4 oz) butter
3 garlic cloves, crushed
1 onion, finely chopped
1 teaspoon lemon juice

To make the anchovy—herb sauce, put all the ingredients in a bowl and stir to combine. If you want a finer sauce, put everything in a blender or food processor and blend until the sauce is smooth. You can also add 1 teaspoon of chopped preserved lemon rind for extra flavour.

To make the smashed potato, cut the potatoes into bite-sized chunks and put them in a saucepan. Cover with cold water and bring to the boil. Cook for 10 minutes, or until the potatoes are tender, then drain. Squash the potatoes a little to break them up.

Meanwhile, thinly slice the kale leaves. Heat the butter in a large heavy-based saucepan over low—medium heat and add the garlic and onion. Cook for about 2 minutes, or until the onion is soft and then add the kale. Cover and cook over medium heat, occasionally stirring the kale to combine it with the onion. When the kale has completely cooked down, add the lemon juice and potatoes and season generously with sea salt and freshly ground black pepper.

Stir all the ingredients together in the pan, then transfer to a serving bowl. Spoon the anchovy—herb sauce over the top.

SERVES 4—6

Porky lentils

More a meal unto itself than a side dish, these porky lentils can also be served alongside sausages or grilled meats as a rich, wintery indulgence. If you remove the pancetta, they make a great vegetarian accompaniment to roast vegetables, such as beetroot or pumpkin, and can be served with a spoonful of goat's curd and a generous drizzle of extra virgin olive oil.

2 tablespoons extra virgin olive oil
100 g (3½ oz) pancetta, finely chopped
1 onion, chopped
2 garlic cloves, crushed
1 celery stalk, sliced
1 fresh bay leaf
2 long red chillies, seeded and finely chopped
210 g (7½ oz/1 cup) puy lentils or tiny blue-green lentils
750 ml (26 fl oz/3 cups) vegetable stock
2 handfuls flat-leaf (Italian) parsley leaves, roughly chopped
goat's curd, to serve (optional)

Heat the olive oil in a heavy-based saucepan over medium heat. Add the pancetta and cook for 2 minutes before adding the onion and garlic. Cook for a further 5 minutes, or until the onion is soft and golden.

Add the celery, bay leaf, chilli and lentils and stir for 1 minute before adding the stock. Bring to the boil, then reduce the heat and simmer for 30 minutes, uncovered, or until the lentils are cooked through. Fold the chopped parsley through the cooked lentils. If you like, top with small spoonfuls of soft goat's curd or crumble some goat's cheese over the top before serving.

SERVES 4–6

Roast cauliflower and brussels sprouts

If you've never had roast or fried brussels sprouts, then you have to try this recipe. If you have had them, then you already know that they can be a wondrous vegetable when treated with love and care and not boiled to a soft, sad mess. In this recipe I've tossed them in some oily Indian spices and roasted them to a burnished crispness.

800 g (1 lb 12 oz) cauliflower
500 g (1 lb 2 oz) brussels sprouts
80 ml (2½ fl oz/⅓ cup) olive oil
2 teaspoons mustard seeds
2 teaspoons nigella seeds
1 teaspoon ground turmeric
1 teaspoon garam masala
1 teaspoon sea salt
½ teaspoon ground white pepper
2 tablespoons lemon juice
1 handful coriander (cilantro) leaves

Preheat the oven to 180°C (350°F). Line a baking tray with baking paper.

Remove and discard the thick stem from the cauliflower and then quarter the cauliflower before cutting it into 1 cm (½ inch) thick slices. Trim the brussels sprouts and then cut them in half lengthways.

Put the olive oil and spices in a large bowl and stir to combine. Add the cauliflower and brussels sprouts and gently turn them in the bowl, to thoroughly coat in the spiced oil.

Transfer the vegetables to the prepared tray. Turn all the sprouts over so that the cut surface is face down. Place the tray in the oven and roast for 50 minutes, or until the cauliflower is dark golden and the sprouts are quite crispy on the outside.

Transfer the roasted vegetables to a serving plate. Drizzle with the lemon juice and sprinkle with the coriander leaves.

SERVES 4–6

Spicy roast sweet potato wedges

80 ml (2 1/2 fl oz/1/3 cup) olive oil
2 tablespoons Cajun spice mix
1 large red chilli, seeded and finely chopped
2 large orange sweet potatoes (1 kg/2 lb 4 oz in total)

Preheat the oven to 200°C (400°F). Line a baking tray with baking paper.

In a large bowl, combine the olive oil, spice mix and chilli. Peel the sweet potatoes and cut them in half crossways, then cut lengthways into thick wedges. Toss the wedges in the seasoned oil.

Put the sweet potato wedges on the prepared tray. Roast for 45 minutes, turning once after 20 minutes, until browned and cooked through.

SERVES 4

Roast pumpkin wedges with spiced pumpkin seeds

800 g (1 lb 12 oz) kent or jap pumpkin (winter squash)
60 ml (2 fl oz/1/4 cup) extra virgin olive oil
1 teaspoon sumac
1 teaspoon ground cumin
1 teaspoon sesame seeds
1 teaspoon nigella seeds

Preheat the oven to 200°C (400°F). Line two large baking trays with baking paper.

Scoop the seeds out of the inside of the pumpkin and reserve them to use later. Cut the pumpkin into 3 cm (1 1/4 inch) wide wedges and put them on one of the prepared trays. Drizzle with 1 tablespoon of the olive oil and then rub the oil over the surface of the wedges. Season with a little sea salt and freshly ground black pepper. Roast in the oven for 40 minutes, or until cooked through.

Meanwhile, rinse the pumpkin seeds in a colander and remove any of the flesh that is still sticking to the seeds. Put the seeds in a bowl with the sumac, cumin, sesame seeds and nigella seeds. Season with sea salt and add 1 tablespoon of olive oil. Stir the seeds together, then lay them on the remaining tray. Roast for 5 minutes, or until golden and fragrant.

Arrange the pumpkin wedges on a serving platter. Scatter with the spiced pumpkin seeds and serve drizzled with the remaining olive oil.

SERVES 4–6

If you haven't already guessed, I'm rather fond of a roast vegetable, and these two recipes capture some of my favourite combinations of earthy spices and mildly sweet vegetables.

The sweet potato wedges work beautifully with roast pork or grilled beef. The pumpkin can be served as a side dish to chicken or roast lamb, or serve them with rocket leaves and a dollop of yoghurt.

Carrot and mint salad

Easy-to-make, sweet and fresh-flavoured, this Moroccan-style salad can be served alongside grilled chicken or lamb. It's a dish that celebrates the carrot and allows it to be centre stage rather than the humble support act it usually is.

2 red onions, thinly sliced
2 tablespoons extra virgin olive oil
1/2 teaspoon ground coriander
400 g (14 oz) carrots, peeled and grated
35 g (1¼ oz/⅓ cup) flaked almonds, toasted
10 mint leaves, finely chopped
2 tablespoons fresh orange juice
1 teaspoon rosewater
70 g (2½ oz) feta cheese
1 handful coriander (cilantro) leaves

Put the onion, olive oil and ground coriander in a frying pan over medium heat and cook for about 10 minutes, or until the onion is caramelised. Transfer to a large bowl and season with sea salt and freshly ground black pepper.

Add the carrot, almonds, mint leaves, orange juice and rosewater and toss to combine. Spoon into a serving bowl and crumble the feta over the top. Garnish with the coriander leaves.

SERVES 4

Warm salad of braised vegetables and barley

Onions, carrots, celery and garlic form the base of most European dishes in one way or another. It's that magical combination of flavours, which, when cooked together, provides a kind of culinary harmony upon which other flavours are pegged—in this case, sweet pumpkin, earthy cumin, tangy lemon and the robust and mostly underrated charm of pearl barley.

Serve this alongside any winter roast or spoon it into pasta bowls and top with grilled sausages for a hearty meal.

100 g (3½ oz/½ cup) pearl barley
½ teaspoon salt
2 red onions, diced
800 g (1 lb 12 oz) kent or jap pumpkin (winter squash), peeled and diced
300 g (10½ oz/1 bunch) dutch (baby) carrots, trimmed, scrubbed and sliced
2 celery stalks, sliced
1 garlic clove, finely chopped
1 teaspoon ground cumin
60 ml (2 fl oz/¼ cup) extra virgin olive oil
1 tablespoon finely chopped curly parsley
1 teaspoon lemon juice

Preheat the oven to 180°C (350°F). Put the barley in a saucepan with 1.5 litres (52 fl oz/6 cups) water. Add the salt and bring to the boil, then reduce the heat to low and simmer for 45 minutes.

Put the onion, pumpkin, carrot and celery in a large roasting tin. Add the garlic, cumin and olive oil, season with sea salt and freshly ground black pepper and cover with foil. Roast in the oven for 40 minutes.

Drain the barley. Remove the vegetables from the oven and stir the barley through the vegetables. Transfer to a large serving bowl and stir in the parsley and lemon juice.

SERVES 4–6

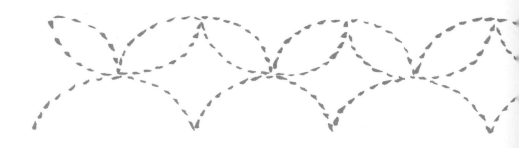

Roast chilli and feta salad

Many, many years ago, when I was backpacking through Greece, I reached the Italian border and swore I'd never again eat another roast capsicum—or any other roasted vegetable! But now I look at this oregano-tinged salad of roast chillies and creamy feta and I find myself not only nostalgic for white cliffs and blue seas but also very hungry.

Banana chillies are great for this recipe because they have a slightly sweet flavour and only a mild chilli kick, so they won't overpower the flavours of the other ingredients.

6 red banana or bullhorn chillies (peppers)
6 green banana or bullhorn chillies (peppers)
125 ml (4 fl oz/$\frac{1}{2}$ cup) extra virgin olive oil
2 tablespoons balsamic vinegar
1 garlic clove, thinly sliced
1 teaspoon dried Greek oregano
6 large basil leaves
1 tablespoon small salted capers, rinsed
75 g (2$\frac{1}{2}$ oz/$\frac{1}{2}$ cup) pitted kalamata olives
120 g (4$\frac{1}{4}$ oz) creamy feta cheese

Heat the grill (broiler) to high. Cut the chillies in half lengthways and arrange on a large baking tray, skin side up, and place under the hot grill. Grill (broil) until the skin is blistered all over. Transfer to a large bowl and cover with plastic wrap, then set aside until cool. Rub the blackened skins from the chillies and then remove the stalks and seeds.

Cut the chillies in half lengthways again and place in a deep serving dish. Whisk together the olive oil and vinegar in a bowl, then add the garlic, oregano, basil, capers and olives. Stir to combine, then pour the dressing over the chillies. Cover the dish with plastic wrap and refrigerate until ready to serve.

Just before serving, crumble the feta over the salad. Serve with a side dish of radicchio or rocket (arugula) leaves.

SERVES 4–6

Bean salad

Simple and delicious, this salad celebrates the beautiful bean in its many forms. The blanched green beans bring a lovely freshness, while the tinned white beans give the salad some substance.

It's a great side dish alongside any type of meat, however you could serve it as a main dish with the addition of grilled and sliced lamb fillet, chunks of tinned tuna or some pan-fried haloumi cheese.

200 g (7 oz) green beans, trimmed and halved lengthways
400 g (14 oz) tinned cannellini beans, drained and rinsed
1/2 red onion, thinly sliced
1 handful flat-leaf (Italian) parsley leaves
1 tablespoon lemon juice
80 ml (2^1/2 fl oz/^{1}/3 cup) extra virgin olive oil

Bring a saucepan of water to the boil and blanch the green beans for about 2 minutes, or until they are emerald green. Drain and rinse under cold running water.

Put the beans in a salad bowl along with the cannellini beans, onion, parsley, lemon juice and olive oil. Season with sea salt and freshly ground black pepper and gently toss together.

SERVES 4

pretty spoons

Berries with coconut crunch

It may be gluten free and dairy free, but this dessert still manages to feel indulgent. I've served the crunch with mixed summer berries, but you could just as easily make a beautiful tropical fruit salad or, if it's winter, serve the crunch with baked apples or pears.

45 g (1½ oz/½ cup) desiccated coconut
45 g (1½ oz/⅓ cup) slivered almonds, roughly chopped
50 g (1¾ oz/¼ cup) finely grated palm sugar (jaggery) or light brown sugar
2 tablespoons coconut oil
250 g (9 oz/1 punnet) strawberries, hulled and halved
125 g (4½ oz/1 punnet) blueberries
125 g (4½ oz/1 punnet) raspberries
160 ml (5¼ fl oz) coconut cream

Preheat the oven to 180°C (350°F). To make the coconut crunch, put the coconut, almonds and palm sugar in a bowl and add the coconut oil. Using your fingertips, work the oil into the other ingredients until it is well incorporated.

Scatter the crunch mixture over a small baking tray and bake for about 10 minutes, or until golden brown. Remove and set aside to cool.

Divide the berries between four bowls and top with the coconut crunch. Spoon the coconut cream over the top.

SERVES 4

Cranberry jelly with mascarpone cream

I've used powdered gelatine in this recipe because it's universally available. However, I do prefer to use sheet gelatine and if you do too, then just follow the manufacturer's instructions for the setting ratio of liquid to gelatine.

These jellies are like mini individual trifles, minus the soggy sponge. The jelly needs to set before you can add the mascarpone topping, so it's a good idea to make the jelly in the morning or the day before.

The mascarpone cream is ridiculously delicious and I often serve it dolloped into bowls with biscotti on the side. A shot glass of liqueur completes the story. Dip the biscotti in the liqueur, top with a spoonful of cream and enjoy.

JELLY
600 ml (21 fl oz) cranberry juice
1 cinnamon stick
4 tablespoons caster (superfine) sugar
1 orange
3 teaspoons powdered gelatine

MASCARPONE CREAM
1 large free-range egg, separated
1$^{1}/_{2}$ tablespoons caster (superfine) sugar
125 g (4$^{1}/_{2}$ oz) mascarpone cheese, at room temperature
1 tablespoon Tia Maria liqueur
1 tablespoon Marsala

fresh raspberries, to serve

Put the cranberry juice in a saucepan with the cinnamon stick and sugar. Slice a few strips of rind from the orange and add them to the pan before juicing the orange and adding the juice to the pan. Bring to the boil, stirring to dissolve the sugar. Remove from the heat.

Put 125 ml (4 fl oz/$^{1}/_{2}$ cup) cold water in a bowl and sprinkle over the gelatine. Strain the cranberry juice into a measuring jug and ensure you have 600 ml (21 fl oz) of liquid. Stir the softened gelatine into the warm liquid and continue to stir for 1 minute, or until the gelatine has completely dissolved. Pour the jelly into six dessert glasses and refrigerate overnight.

On the following day, make the mascarpone cream. Using a whisk, beat the egg white in a clean bowl until soft peaks form. Add the sugar and continue to whisk until the egg white is firm and glossy.

In a separate bowl, stir together the egg yolk, mascarpone, Tia Maria and Marsala. Fold half the egg white into the mascarpone mixture until well combined, then gently fold through the remaining half.

Spoon the mascarpone cream over the jelly and place in the fridge until ready to serve. Top with fresh raspberries before serving.

SERVES 6

Little pavlovas with passionfruit and banana

If it has meringue, whipped cream and fresh fruit then I'm there ... no matter what the version. These are individual pavlovas topped with passionfruit and banana and flavoured with raw sugar and balsamic vinegar. This does make them a soft golden colour, so if you want your meringues white, then replace with white caster sugar and white wine vinegar.

3 large free-range egg whites
150 g (5½ oz) raw (or golden) caster (superfine) sugar
½ teaspoon balsamic vinegar
¼ teaspoon cream of tartar
1 teaspoon cornflour (cornstarch)
1 teaspoon vanilla bean paste
300 ml (10½ fl oz) cream, whipped
3 ripe bananas, sliced
pulp of 6 passionfruit
icing (confectioners') sugar, for dusting

Preheat the oven to 150°C (300°F). Line a baking tray with baking paper.

Using an electric mixer, whisk the egg whites until they form soft peaks. Gradually add the sugar, beating continuously until the meringue is firm and glossy. Add the vinegar, cream of tartar, cornflour and vanilla bean paste and beat for a further 1 minute.

Spoon the meringue onto the prepared tray to form six big dollops and then use the back of the spoon to make a hollow in the centre of each.

Bake for 10 minutes, then reduce the oven temperature to 120°C (235°F) and bake for a further 1 hour. Turn the oven off and leave the pavlovas in the oven, with the door slightly ajar, to cool for 30 minutes.

Serve the pavlovas topped with some whipped cream, sliced banana, passionfruit and a dusting of icing sugar.

SERVES 6

Here are a few other flavour combinations for the pavlovas using the basic recipe on the opposite page:

~ For a summery tropical treat, finely dice banana, peach, mango, papaya and pineapple. Add some passionfruit and a little lime juice and stir to combine. Top the pavlovas with crème fraîche and spoon over the fruit salsa.

~ For a berry pavlova, replace the balsamic vinegar with white wine vinegar and the vanilla bean paste with rosewater. After baking, top with whipped cream and mixed berries.

~ For a richer wintery version, dust the uncooked meringues with a little dutch cocoa before baking. Serve with whipped cream, bottled morello cherries and a drizzle of melted chocolate.

~ Scatter shredded coconut over the meringues before they go into the oven and serve with sweetened plain yoghurt and sliced mango.

~ If you love Asian flavours, replace the cornflour (cornstarch) with green tea powder and top the baked pavlovas with mango and lychees.

If you have a crowd coming over, these are a fun, no-stress way to present dessert. Make a couple of batches of the pavlovas and serve them stacked, like a beautiful display in a French patisserie window, with generous bowls of whipped cream and fruit to the side.

Mandarin granita

For some reason, when it comes to desserts, the mandarin is a somewhat unloved and mostly forgotten fruit and yet its lovely perfumed citrus flavour can occasionally make a nice change from the usual oranges and lemons.

If I'm rational about it, I know it's because mandarin skin doesn't lend itself to zesting, it isn't as easy to juice as an orange, and its segmented nature means that it isn't easy to slice, but its flavour is worth celebrating. So, start juicing and make this granita, which is perfect to serve after a particularly rich meal—or if you ever find yourself making a citrus syrup to pour over a cake, make a mandarin version as an unexpected twist.

220 g (7³/4 oz/1 cup) caster (superfine) sugar
375 ml (13 fl oz/1¹/2 cups) fresh mandarin juice
2 tablespoons lime juice
60 ml (2 fl oz/¹/4 cup) dark rum
90 g (3¹/4 oz/¹/2 cup) pomegranate arils, to serve

Put the sugar in a saucepan with 750 ml (26 fl oz/3 cups) water. Bring to the boil, then reduce the heat and simmer for 5 minutes, stirring once or twice to ensure the sugar has dissolved. Remove the pan from the heat and cool.

When the syrup is cool, stir in the mandarin juice, lime juice and rum. Pour into a shallow metal container and freeze for 1 hour.

Using a fork, scrape the ice from around the edges back into the liquid, then return to the freezer. Repeat this process another three times, or until the granita looks like crushed ice.

To serve, spoon the granita into six chilled dessert glasses and top with the pomegranate arils.

SERVES 6

Meringue roulade with rhubarb

I think rhubarb is a little like Vegemite. If you grew up eating it, you can't imagine life without it, but if it wasn't a part of your childhood, then you tend to steer away from that strange vegetable masquerading as a fruit.

When I was a child, everyone had rhubarb growing in their garden, so there was always a glass bowl of velvety, sweet rhubarb in the refrigerator, ready to be spooned over ice cream, custard or, if you had a sweet tooth like my grandfather, on buttered bread. It was only as an adult that I discovered you could roast it and cook it with possibly a little less sugar! In this recipe, the sweetness of the meringue is nicely balanced by the slight tartness of the rhubarb.

350 g (12 oz) rhubarb, finely chopped
250 g (9 oz) caster (superfine) sugar
1 teaspoon rosewater
5 large free-range egg whites
2 teaspoons cornflour (cornstarch)
1 teaspoon natural vanilla extract
1 teaspoon white wine vinegar
45 g (1½ oz/⅓ cup) pistachio nuts
200 ml (7 fl oz) thickened cream, whipped
icing (confectioners') sugar, for dusting

Preheat the oven to 180°C (350°F). Line two baking trays with baking paper. Draw a 25 x 35 cm (10 x 14 inch) rectangle on the back of one sheet of paper, for the meringue.

Put the rhubarb and 75 g (2½ oz/⅓ cup) of the sugar in a bowl and add the rosewater. Stir to combine, then put the rhubarb on the prepared tray. Cover with baking paper and foil and bake for 30 minutes. Remove and set aside to cool.

Meanwhile, using an electric mixer, whisk the egg whites until they form soft peaks, then slowly add the remaining sugar and whisk until the sugar has dissolved and the mixture is smooth and glossy. Fold in the cornflour, vanilla and vinegar. Using the marked rectangle on the paper as a guide, spread the meringue evenly over the tray. Bake for 20 minutes.

Put the pistachios in a small food processor and blend to a fine texture. Spread the ground pistachios over a large sheet of baking paper. Remove the meringue from the oven and flip it over onto the baking paper, so the meringue is sitting on the ground pistachios. With the short side facing you, roll the meringue and baking paper up, like a Swiss (jelly) roll. Set aside to cool for 15 minutes, then unroll and transfer to a long piece of plastic wrap. The meringue may have cracked a little, but don't panic as the cream makes a wonderful mortar.

Spread the whipped cream evenly over the meringue, leaving 3 cm (1¼ inches) clear at one end, and then cover with the cooled rhubarb. Carefully roll the meringue up again using the plastic wrap to keep it smooth and even. When fully rolled, lightly smooth and press the roll into an even log shape. Remove the plastic wrap and transfer the roulade to a serving plate. Dust with icing sugar.

SERVES 6

Spiced yoghurt with grilled figs

Years ago, I was travelling through the Greek islands and stumbled across an early morning market in the centre of a beautiful old town. In one corner, a man was selling the most amazing yoghurt, drizzled with honey, which he served in little terracotta bowls. Across the way was a fruit stall piled high with local figs warming in the morning sunshine. To this day, it is one of my most memorable breakfasts.

The spiced yoghurt can also be served with fresh berries, poached stone fruit, stewed apple or oven-baked rhubarb. If the fruit is a little tart, drizzle some honey over the yoghurt.

SPICED YOGHURT
125 ml (4 fl oz/1/2 cup) thin (pouring/whipping) cream
2 cardamom pods, crushed
1 cinnamon stick
1/2 vanilla bean, halved lengthways
4 thick slices fresh ginger
500 g (1 lb 2 oz) Greek-style yoghurt

6 figs, halved
1 1/2 tablespoons light brown sugar
honey, for drizzling (optional)

To make the spiced yoghurt, put the cream in a small saucepan with the cardamom pods, cinnamon stick, vanilla bean and ginger. Simmer over low heat for 5 minutes, then remove from the heat and set aside to cool.

When cool, strain the spiced cream into a bowl and add the yoghurt. Stir to combine and cover with plastic wrap. Refrigerate until ready to serve.

Heat the grill (broiler) to high. Line a baking tray with baking paper. Put the figs on the prepared tray, cut side up, and press the brown sugar into the cut surface of the figs. Grill (broil) the figs for 4 minutes, or until the sugar starts to bubble and caramelise. Serve the figs with the spiced yoghurt and an optional drizzle of honey.

SERVES 6

Lemon posset with sugared zest

Part of me loves this dessert for its wonderful old-fashioned name but I mostly love how stupidly simple it is. It sets into a sublimely silky, creamy, lemony pudding that could be served with crisp almond bread, but for this recipe I've decided to celebrate the lemon and garnish it with sugared zest. The zest adds just a little bit of sweet texture, which is really all you need, because the posset is pretty darn close to perfection as it is.

Just one quick note: make sure you buy thick, or double, cream and not thickened cream or the result will be disappointing.

3–4 lemons
600 ml (21½ fl oz) thick (double/heavy) cream (48% butterfat)
165 g (5¾ oz/¾ cup) caster (superfine) sugar, plus 110 g (3¾ oz/½ cup) extra, for the sugared zest

Before juicing the lemons for the posset, remove the lemon skin in long julienne strips using a zester. Set to one side. Juice the lemons to give you 125 ml (4 fl oz/½ cup) of lemon juice. Depending on their juiciness, you may only need to use three lemons.

Put the cream and sugar in a saucepan over high heat and bring to the boil, stirring to dissolve the sugar. Reduce the heat to low and simmer, uncovered, for 3 minutes, stirring regularly.

Remove from the heat and stir in the lemon juice; stand for 3 minutes. Strain the cream and lemon mixture into a jug and then pour into six 185 ml (6 fl oz/¾ cup) glasses. When cool, cover with plastic wrap and refrigerate for 4 hours or overnight.

To make the sugared zest, fill a small saucepan with water and add the strips of lemon zest. Bring to the boil, then drain off the water and refill with cold water. Return to the boil, then drain and repeat the process once more. Meanwhile, sprinkle half of the extra sugar over a plate.

After the zest has been boiled for the third time, drain and then carefully transfer the strips from the strainer to the plate of sugar. Sprinkle the remaining sugar over the top and then set aside for 2 hours. Serve the posset topped with the sugared zest.

SERVES 6

Chocolate parfait with coffee prunes and sugary walnuts

I've served this parfait so many times and every time someone asks for the recipe. Let's face it, what's not to love about a rich chocolate ice cream that needs no churning and can be made in advance. This is a winter version, served with slightly alcoholic prunes and walnuts, but you could serve it with fresh berries, candied cumquats, raspberry sauce or almond praline.

125 g (4^{1}/$_{2}$ oz) caster (superfine) sugar
100 g (3^{1}/$_{2}$ oz) dark chocolate (70% cocoa)
4 large free-range egg yolks
2 tablespoons unsweetened cocoa powder
60 ml (2 fl oz/^{1}/$_{4}$ cup) Kahlua
300 g (10^{1}/$_{2}$ oz) sour cream
12 pitted prunes, thinly sliced
60 ml (2 fl oz/^{1}/$_{4}$ cup) hot and strong coffee
115 g (4 oz/1 cup) walnut halves
3 tablespoons icing (confectioners') sugar

Line a 7 x 22 cm (2^{3}/$_{4}$ x 8^{1}/$_{2}$ inch) loaf (bar) tin with baking paper, allowing 5 cm (2 inches) of paper to overhang the two long sides.

Put the sugar and 125 ml (4 fl oz/^{1}/$_{2}$ cup) water in a saucepan. Bring to the boil, stirring until the sugar has dissolved. Boil briskly for 3 minutes, then remove from the heat. Break the chocolate into pieces and add to the hot sugar syrup, stirring until smooth.

Using an electric mixer, whisk the egg yolks until pale, then add the cocoa and whisk until combined. Slowly add the hot chocolate sauce, beating until the mixture has cooled. Stir in 1 tablespoon of the Kahlua, then beat in the sour cream. Spoon the mixture into the prepared tin and freeze overnight.

Put the prunes in a small bowl and pour the hot coffee and remaining Kahlua over the prunes. Cover and set aside until ready to serve.

Put the walnuts in a non-stick frying pan and sprinkle over the icing sugar. Cook over medium heat until the sugar melts and the walnuts begin to caramelise. Remove from the pan.

To serve, turn the parfait out onto a clean board and cut into six slices. Serve with the prunes and caramelised walnuts.

SERVES 6

Pineapple with ginger and cardamom syrup

This is a wonderfully aromatic syrup that you could pour over any combination of tropical fruit, but I think that it's most suited to the slightly acidic nature of pineapple. Serve the chilled syrupy pineapple at the end of a long, hot day, with or without the sorbet, and you'll be met with beaming smiles.

75 g (2½ oz/⅓ cup) sugar
4 cardamom pods, crushed
2 cm (¾ inch) piece fresh ginger, peeled and thinly sliced
1 vanilla bean, halved lengthways
2 tablespoons lime juice
1 fresh pineapple
mint leaves, to serve

Put the sugar, cardamom pods, ginger, vanilla bean and lime juice in a saucepan with 80 ml (2½ fl oz/⅓ cup) water. Bring to the boil and then reduce the heat and simmer until the sugar has dissolved. Set aside to cool before pouring into a jug. Chill until ready to use.

Remove the skin from the pineapple and cut the flesh into 2 cm (¾ inch) dice. Put the pineapple in a bowl and pour over the spiced syrup.

Serve the pineapple salad with fresh mint leaves and, if you like, lime or mango sorbet.

SERVES 6

Flavoured syrups are a great way to add a bit of glamour to a simple fruit salad or a selection of seasonal fruit. They can also be poured over ice cream for a quick midweek dessert or spooned over breakfast yoghurt for a little early morning sugar hit.

Here are a few other flavours:

PASSIONFRUIT AND LIME SYRUP

Put 220 g (7¾ oz/1 cup) sugar and 250 ml (9 fl oz/1 cup) water in a small saucepan. Add 1 small stem of bruised lemongrass and bring to the boil, then reduce the heat and simmer for 5 minutes.

Stir 125 ml (4 fl oz/½ cup) passionfruit pulp into the hot syrup before removing from the heat. When cool, remove the lemongrass from the syrup, add 2 tablespoons lime juice and store in a glass jar or bottle in the refrigerator.

CHILLI AND VANILLA SYRUP

Put 220 g (7¾ oz/1 cup) sugar and 500 ml (17 fl oz/2 cups) water in a small saucepan. Split 1 vanilla bean lengthways. Remove and discard the seeds from 1 long red chilli and finely chop. Add the split vanilla bean and chopped chilli to the pan and bring to the boil, then reduce the heat to low and simmer for 10 minutes. Remove the pan from the heat and leave to cool, then stir in 1 tablespoon lime juice.

Spice-poached quinces

I love the flavour of quince, whether it's poached, as in this recipe, or slow-roasted to ruby perfection in the oven. It's a sweetly perfumed fruit that does take a little bit of time to cook, but the rewards are great.

I have to admit that I also buy quinces for decorative purposes. As soon as they appear in the market, I buy a large bag, of which half is cooked and half is piled into a bowl and put out for display. Their sunny yellowness always makes me smile and they smell amazing.

110 g (3^3/$_4$ oz/^{1}/$_2$ cup) sugar
2 tablespoons honey
2 fresh bay leaves
2 star anise
1 vanilla bean, halved lengthways
3 large quinces
whipped cream, to serve

Put the sugar, honey, bay leaves, star anise and vanilla bean in a saucepan with 500 ml (17 fl oz/2 cups) water. Stir over medium heat until the sugar has dissolved.

Peel the quinces, then cut each one into eighths and core the segments. Add the quince segments to the syrup and add enough water to ensure the quinces are covered in the syrup. Dampen a piece of baking paper with water and press it over the quinces.

Cook over medium heat until the syrup comes to a slow simmer. Reduce the heat to low, cover the pan with a lid and cook for a further 3^1/$_2$ hours, removing the bay leaves after the first hour. When cooked, the quince segments should be soft and the syrup and quinces should be a wonderful rose colour.

Serve the quinces with whipped cream and almond bread or spiced biscotti (page 222). Drizzle some of the quince syrup over the cream.

SERVES 6

Nectarines with creamed rice

The cardamom and orange flower water give this creamed rice a wonderfully exotic flavour that works beautifully with any poached or grilled fruit, and it's a surprisingly light dessert because of the whipped cream. The only problem I have is that if I serve it to less than six people, I'll eat the leftovers cold for breakfast the following morning, with the somewhat farcical belief that because it's rice, it is a second cousin to porridge!

110 g (3¾ oz/½ cup) short-grain white rice
650 ml (22½ fl oz) milk
1 vanilla bean, halved lengthways
¼ teaspoon ground cardamom
2 tablespoons sugar
1 teaspoon orange flower water
125 ml (4 fl oz/½ cup) cream, whipped
6 nectarines, halved
3 tablespoons raw (or golden) caster (superfine) sugar

Rinse the rice in cold water and drain. Put the rice, milk, vanilla bean, cardamom and sugar in a saucepan and stir over medium heat for about 2 minutes, or until the sugar has dissolved. Bring to the boil, reduce the heat to low and simmer gently for 20–25 minutes, stirring occasionally.

When the rice has cooked, remove the vanilla bean and transfer the rice to a bowl. Set aside to cool completely, then stir in the orange flower water and fold the whipped cream into the rice. Cover and chill until ready to serve.

Line a baking tray with baking paper. Put the nectarine halves on the tray, skin side down. Sprinkle with the raw sugar and place under a hot grill (broiler) or in a hot oven. Cook for 5 minutes, or until the sugar begins to caramelise.

Serve the nectarines with a generous spoonful of the creamed rice.

SERVES 6

Poached peaches
with lemon cream

I have wonderful childhood memories of peaches. Every summer my uncle, who had a peach farm, would send my grandfather a couple of boxes of white peaches. They were the first peaches of the season and the boxes were opened with great ceremony. We'd all lean in and inhale the amazing aromas, then my grandfather would set to work poaching, bottling and preserving them for winter. Oh the wonder of those tall glass jars, packed with sweetly poached peaches and filled with the promise of summer flavours.

220 g (7³/4 oz/1 cup) sugar
1 vanilla bean, halved lengthways
4 peaches
1 large free-range egg white
2 tablespoons caster (superfine) sugar
250 g (9 oz) cream cheese, at room temperature
1 tablespoon lemon juice
¹/2 teaspoon vanilla bean paste

To poach the peaches, put the sugar in a saucepan (large enough to fit the four peaches in a single layer) with the vanilla bean and 1 litre (35 fl oz/ 4 cups) water. Stir over medium heat until the sugar has dissolved. Bring to the boil, then reduce the heat to a low simmer.

Lightly score the skin of each peach with a single line around its circumference. Lower the fruit into the syrup and cover with a piece of crumpled baking paper. Simmer for 3–5 minutes, or until the peaches are tender, rolling the fruit over halfway through cooking.

Remove the peaches with a slotted spoon and transfer to a bowl. Bring the syrup to the boil and cook, uncovered, until reduced by one-third. Pour the syrup over the peaches and chill until ready to serve.

Meanwhile, to make the lemon cream, put the egg white in a clean bowl and whisk with an electric mixer until firm. Slowly add the caster sugar and continue to whisk until the egg white is stiff and glossy.

Put the cream cheese in a separate bowl with the lemon juice and vanilla bean paste and beat until smooth. Fold the egg white into the cream cheese in two batches and stir until well combined. Cover and chill until ready to serve.

Serve the poached peaches with the lemon cream.

SERVES 4

A perfectly poached peach, with its golden sunset hues, is a beautiful thing to behold and to eat.

Chocolate and chestnut mousse

I first tasted sweet chestnut purée years ago in a café in Paris and, along with chestnuts roasted on the street over smoky coals, they became but a distant memory of great trips abroad until, hooray, Australia started growing its own chestnuts and finally started producing its own purées.

This is a very simple chocolate mousse that I've topped with shop-bought sweet chestnut purée. The combination makes for a truly decadent dessert—but you do need to serve it with a bit of whipped cream, to bring all the flavours together.

100 g (3¹/₂ oz) dark chocolate (70% cocoa), chopped
2 tablespoons brandy
3 large free-range eggs, separated
120 g (4¹/₄ oz) sweet chestnut purée
150 ml (5 fl oz) cream, whipped

Put the chopped chocolate and brandy in a heatproof bowl over a saucepan of simmering water, ensuring the base of the bowl does not touch the water. Stir occasionally until the chocolate has melted and is smooth, then remove the bowl from the heat.

Add the egg yolks, one at a time, beating in each one with a wooden spoon until it is well incorporated. The chocolate will seize and stiffen at first but should be smooth and glossy by the time you have added the third yolk. If not, add a tablespoon of cream to the mixture to loosen it a little.

Using an electric mixer, whisk the egg whites in a clean, dry bowl until they form stiff peaks. Add one-third of the egg white to the chocolate and gently fold to combine. Add another third and gently work it into the mixture before adding the final third of the whites. The mixture should be quite smooth and uniform in colour.

Spoon the mixture into six bowls or glasses. Cover with plastic wrap and refrigerate for several hours or overnight.

To serve, top each mousse with a tablespoon of chestnut purée, then add a generous spoonful of whipped cream.

SERVES 6

Tea-scented pashka

This is a glorious old-fashioned dessert that was traditionally served as part of Russian Easter celebrations. It's definitely one for a crowd as it's very rich and not worth doing in smaller quantities, so keep it for special occasions or a long Easter Sunday lunch.

You can make it in any bowl or mould, but for visual impact it really is worthwhile finding and investing in a beautiful old-style jelly mould.

3 Earl Grey tea bags
125 ml (4 fl oz/1/2 cup) boiling water
55 g (2 oz/1/4 cup) finely chopped glacé ginger
75 g (2 1/2 oz/1/2 cup) currants
95 g (3 1/4 oz/1/2 cup) finely chopped dried figs
70 g (2 1/2 oz/1/2 cup) chopped dried cranberries
2 tablespoons finely grated lemon zest
2 tablespoons finely grated orange zest
2 tablespoons lemon juice
1 tablespoon Marsala
100 g (3 1/2 oz) unsalted butter, softened
90 g (3 1/4 oz/1/2 cup) raw (or golden) caster (superfine) sugar
2 large free-range egg yolks
500 g (1 lb 2 oz) fresh full-fat ricotta cheese
250 g (9 oz) mascarpone
70 g (2 1/2 oz/1/2 cup) pistachio nuts, toasted and roughly chopped

---

Line a 2 litre (70 fl oz/8 cup) capacity jelly mould or bowl with muslin (cheesecloth), allowing it to drape over the sides. The muslin helps to draw away any excess liquid and also helps to ease the pashka out of the mould.

Steep the tea bags in the boiling water for 30 minutes while you prepare all the ingredients.

Mix the ginger, currants, figs, cranberries, lemon zest, orange zest, lemon juice and Marsala in a bowl and add the tea. Set aside to marinate for 30 minutes.

Using an electric mixer, cream the butter and sugar until pale, then add the egg yolks, one at a time, beating after each addition. Add the ricotta in heaped spoonfuls, beating it into the mixture. Fold in the mascarpone.

Fold the soaked fruit and pistachios through the ricotta mixture. Spoon the mixture into the prepared mould and fold the muslin over the top. Cover and refrigerate overnight.

Turn the pashka out onto a serving plate and serve in thin wedges, with tiny cups of espresso coffee or dessert wine.

SERVES 12

Hazelnut meringue with berries

I've scattered a few old favourites through this book and this recipe is from one of my first cookbooks. It's become one of those go-to recipes when I find myself wondering what to make for dessert and so I thought it was definitely worth revisiting, as it never fails to garner attention and is always gobbled up whenever I serve it. Nutty meringue, whipped cream and berries ... what's not to love?

2 free-range egg whites
110 g (3³/4 oz/¹/2 cup) caster (superfine) sugar
4 tablespoons ground hazelnuts
300 ml (10¹/2 fl oz) thickened (whipping) cream
1 teaspoon vanilla bean paste
500 g (1 lb 2 oz) mixed berries, such as strawberries, raspberries and blueberries
icing (confectioners') sugar, for dusting

Preheat the oven to 150°C (300°F). Line two baking trays with baking paper. Draw a 20 cm (8 inch) circle on the back of each sheet of paper.

Using an electric mixer, whisk the egg whites in a clean, dry bowl until they form soft peaks. Slowly add the sugar, continuing to whisk until the mixture is stiff and glossy. Fold in the ground hazelnuts.

Divide the meringue between the two marked rounds on the prepared trays. Using the back of a spoon, spread the mixture out until you have two smooth circles of meringue. Bake for 40 minutes. Turn the oven off and leave the meringues in the oven, with the door slightly ajar, to cool for 30 minutes.

Meanwhile, whip the cream and fold in the vanilla bean paste. Prepare the berries. If using strawberries, remove the stalks and cut them in half or into quarters, depending on their size.

When the meringues are cool, put one of the rounds on a serving plate and top with half the cream and half the berries. When placing the berries into the cream, remember that you need to make a flat surface for the second meringue.

Top the berry layer with the second meringue and spoon over the remaining cream. Arrange the remaining berries on top and dust with icing sugar.

SERVES 6

Bay-baked pears with chocolate ice cream

In this dessert, the pears do all the hard work. As they are roasting, their flesh is melding with the magical combination of butter, bay leaf, brown sugar and Marsala—and then they just sit back while we cover them in cream and serve with chocolate ice cream. In winter, desserts don't get much easier.

6 small pears, such as corella or josephine
40 g (1½ oz) unsalted butter, softened
125 ml (4 fl oz/½ cup) Marsala
3 tablespoons light brown sugar
2 bay leaves
chocolate ice cream, to serve
thin (pouring/whipping) cream, to serve

Preheat the oven to 180°C (350°F). Halve the pears, then use a teaspoon to scoop out the cores. Place the pears, skin side up, on a cutting board. Using a sharp knife, cut a thin slice from the top of the rounded side of each pear (this will give them a flat surface to sit on).

Put the pears on a shallow baking tray, skin side down. Rub the butter over the top of the pears.

Put the Marsala and brown sugar in a small bowl and stir until the sugar has dissolved. Spoon a little of the sweetened Marsala into the hollowed cores of the pears, and then pour the rest into the tray. Add the bay leaves to the tray, cover with foil and bake for 1 hour.

Serve the pears warm or at room temperature with the chocolate ice cream. Drizzle the pears with a little cream and some of the juices left in the tray.

SERVES 6

teacups and
cake plates

Biscotti

I've been making these biscotti for years. I always make a double batch and then store them in several airtight jars in the pantry, so it feels like I have an endless supply for nibbling on or giving away as spur-of-the-moment gifts.

I like to slice the biscotti as thinly as I can, making them easier to eat than your standard shop-bought version, but you do need a very sharp bread knife to do this, and a steady hand. Serve these as an afternoon snack with a cup of tea or alongside a creamy dessert at night.

150 g (5¹/2 oz/1 cup) self-raising flour
110 g (3³/4 oz/¹/2 cup) caster (superfine) sugar
65 g (2¹/4 oz/1 cup) shredded coconut
145 g (5 oz/1 cup) dried cranberries
75 g (2¹/2 oz/¹/2 cup) currants
115 g (4 oz/³/4 cup) pistachio nuts
¹/2 teaspoon ground cinnamon
¹/2 teaspoon ground allspice
finely grated zest of 1 orange
3 large free-range eggs, beaten

Preheat the oven to 180°C (350°F). Line a baking tray with baking paper.

Put all the ingredients, except the beaten egg, in a large bowl. Stir to coat the fruit and nuts evenly in the flour.

Make a well in the centre and add the beaten egg. Fold the egg into the ingredients to make a sticky dough. At this point, I find it easier to get my hands in and work the ingredients together as the mixture is very firm and almost feels as if it won't come together. If you keep persevering, as you would when making a stiff bread dough, it will finally form a solid, cohesive lump.

Turn out the dough onto a clean, floured work surface. Divide the mixture into two portions, then roll each portion into a log about 4 cm (1¹/2 inches) in diameter. Sit the logs on the prepared tray, leaving some space between them to allow for spreading. Bake for 30 minutes, or until firm to the touch, then remove from the oven and cool on a wire rack.

Reduce the oven temperature to 140°C (275°F). Using a very sharp bread knife, cut each loaf into thin slices about 5 mm (¹/4 inch) thick. I usually slice mine on the diagonal to give a longer, more elegant shape. Spread the biscotti onto two baking trays and bake for 20 minutes, turning the biscotti halfway through cooking.

Remove from the oven and cool on wire racks. When cool, store in an airtight container until ready to serve.

MAKES ABOUT 50

Banana and date bundt cake

If you don't already have one, it really is worth investing in a bundt tin, not only for this rather large and glorious cake, but for any large cake recipe. Bundt tins come in a range of beautiful moulded shapes and will make even the simplest of cakes look magical.

This cake is richly flavoured with banana and dates and is finished with a gooey caramel coconut glaze—strong flavours that are majestic enough to match its right royal shape.

200 g (7 oz) fresh dates, pitted and chopped
125 g (4 1/2 oz) unsalted butter, diced
1 teaspoon bicarbonate of soda (baking soda)
125 ml (4 fl oz/1/2 cup) boiling water
185 g (6 1/2 oz/1 cup, lightly packed) light brown sugar
2 large ripe bananas (350 g/12 oz), mashed
3 large free-range eggs, beaten
130 g (4 1/2 oz/1/2 cup) Greek-style yoghurt
300 g (10 1/2 oz/2 cups) plain (all-purpose) flour
1 tablespoon baking powder
1 teaspoon salt

CARAMEL GLAZE
220 g (7 3/4 oz/1 cup) caster (superfine) sugar
50 g (1 3/4 oz) unsalted butter
a pinch of salt
140 ml (4 3/4 fl oz) coconut cream

Preheat the oven to 180°C (350°F). Generously grease and flour an 8 cm (3 1/4 inch) deep, 24 cm (9 1/2 inch) fluted bundt (ring) tin.

Put the chopped dates in a large bowl with the butter and bicarbonate of soda. Add the boiling water and stir until the butter has melted. Add the brown sugar and mashed banana, then the eggs and yoghurt and stir well to combine. Sift the flour, baking powder and salt over the batter and gently fold together.

Spoon the batter into the prepared tin and bake for 40–45 minutes, or until a skewer inserted into the centre of the cake comes out clean. Cool in the tin for 10 minutes before turning out onto a wire rack.

To make the caramel glaze, put the sugar, butter and salt in a saucepan over medium heat and cook for 4 minutes. When the butter and sugar start to melt together and combine, begin to stir the mixture until the caramel is dark brown.

Remove from the heat and add the coconut cream. Hold the pan away from you as you do this, as the caramel will splutter quite a bit. Stir to combine, then pour the hot mixture into a mixing bowl and continue to stir until the caramel begins to cool. When it feels quite thick, drizzle the caramel glaze over the cake. Allow the caramel to set before serving.

SERVES 12

Coconut and banana bread

Many years ago I worked in a café where this bread was one of the favourite breakfast items on the menu. I've played with the recipe ever since. Back then it was served toasted with sliced banana, but because I often find myself with a couple of overripe bananas in need of a good baking, I've popped them into the bread instead.

The recipe was originally baked as little cakes, so if your children love the flavour of this bread, you could also make lunchbox muffins by spooning the batter into small muffin cases and baking them for about 15 minutes, or until cooked through.

100 g (3½ oz/1½ cups) shredded coconut
250 ml (9 fl oz/1 cup) buttermilk
2 ripe bananas, mashed
100 g (3½ oz) unsalted butter, melted
2 teaspoons ground cinnamon
½ teaspoon ground cardamom
1 large free-range egg, lightly beaten
110 g (3¾ oz/½ cup) sugar
225 g (8 oz/1½ cups) self-raising flour, sifted

Preheat the oven to 180°C (350°F). Lightly grease a 9 x 20 cm (3½ x 8 inch) loaf (bar) tin and line the base and sides with baking paper.

Put the coconut in a large bowl and pour in the buttermilk. Stir to combine and then leave to sit for 10 minutes. Add the remaining ingredients to the bowl and stir well to combine.

Spoon the batter into the prepared tin and bake for 1 hour, or until a skewer inserted into the centre of the bread comes out clean. Allow the bread to cool a little in the tin before turning out onto a serving plate. Serve warm or toasted with butter.

SERVES 8–10

Cinnamon and cherry olive oil cake

This cake is slightly sponge-like in texture and it's always a surprise that it carries the weight of the cherries. I use bottled morello cherries because they have such a lovely sweet sourness and they can be sourced year round. They usually come with the seeds removed, but check them carefully before you add them to the base of the tin—an unexpected cherry seed comes as an unwelcome addition to any cake.

680 g (1 lb 8 oz) bottled morello cherries
3 large free-range eggs
330 g (11½ oz/1½ cups) caster (superfine) sugar
1 tablespoon finely grated orange zest
125 ml (4 fl oz/½ cup) extra virgin olive oil
300 g (10½ oz/2 cups) plain (all-purpose) flour
1 teaspoon baking powder
1 teaspoon ground cinnamon, plus extra for dusting
300 ml (10½ fl oz) thickened cream, whipped

Preheat the oven to 180°C (350°F). Lightly grease a 22 cm (8½ inch) square cake tin and line the base and sides with baking paper.

Drain the cherries, reserving the liquid, and then arrange the cherries over the base of the tin.

Using an electric mixer, beat the eggs, 275 g (9¾ oz/1¼ cups) of the sugar and the orange zest for about 5 minutes, or until thick and creamy. Add the olive oil and beat for a further 1 minute. Sift the flour and baking powder over the egg mixture and gently fold to combine.

Pour the batter over the cherries in the tin. Using a spatula, smooth the top of the batter, drawing the mixture up at the sides a little. Bake for about 40 minutes, or until a skewer inserted into the centre of the cake comes out clean. Remove from the oven and leave to cool in the tin.

Meanwhile, put the reserved liquid from the cherries, the remaining 55 g (3 oz/¼ cup) of sugar and the cinnamon in a small saucepan. Bring to the boil, then reduce the heat and simmer, uncovered, for 5–10 minutes, or until the liquid has reduced by half.

Turn the cake upside down onto a serving plate and spoon the syrup over the cake. Top with the whipped cream and dust with extra cinnamon.

SERVES 8–10

Lemon syrup cake

If you love intense lemony flavours, then this is the cake for you. The slightly dense almond meal cake batter is tinged with lemon zest, the cooked cake is soaked in lemon syrup and, finally, drizzled with a lemon glaze. It might seem like I've gone a bit overboard on the lemon, but the end result is truly sublime.

150 g (5¹/2 oz) unsalted butter, softened
1 teaspoon natural vanilla extract
2 teaspoons finely grated lemon zest
330 g (11¹/2 oz/1¹/2 cups) caster (superfine) sugar
3 large free-range eggs
200 g (7 oz/2 cups) almond meal
110 g (3³/4 oz/3/4 cup) self-raising flour, sifted
80 ml (2¹/2 fl oz/¹/3 cup) lemon juice

LEMON GLAZE
125 g (4¹/2 oz/1 cup) icing (confectioners') sugar, sifted
1¹/2 tablespoons lemon juice, approximately

Preheat the oven to 160°C (315°F). Lightly grease a 22 cm (8¹/2 inch) spring-form cake tin and line the base and side with baking paper.

Using an electric mixer, beat the butter, vanilla, lemon zest and 220 g (7³/4 oz/1 cup) of the caster sugar in a small bowl until light and fluffy. Beat in the eggs, one at a time, until well combined. Stir in the almond meal and sifted flour. Spread the mixture into the prepared tin and smooth the top with a spatula. Bake for 1 hour, or until a skewer inserted into the centre of the cake comes out clean.

Meanwhile, combine the remaining 110 g (3³/4 oz/¹/2 cup) of caster sugar and the lemon juice in a small saucepan over medium heat, stirring until the sugar has dissolved. Remove from the heat.

Using a fine skewer, poke small holes all over the surface of the hot cake. Pour the hot lemon syrup over the cake and leave the cake in the tin to cool and soak up the syrup.

To make the lemon glaze, combine the sifted icing sugar and lemon juice in a small bowl and stir until smooth. Remove the cake from the tin and carefully transfer to a serving plate. Drizzle the lemon glaze over the top.

SERVES 8–10

For me, this is the perfect cake to serve for afternoon tea. It's indulgent, without being too rich, and the flavours work beautifully with a cup of tea.

Orange and pistachio cake

With its indulgent cream cheese icing, this cake owes a lot to that perennial café favourite of the late-twentieth century, the carrot cake. However, minus the carrot it's a bit less earnest, a little lighter in flavour and texture, and not nearly as predictable. In fact, orange and pistachio are great culinary companions and work beautifully alongside the soft richness of the cream cheese.

90 g (3¼ oz/⅔ cup) pistachio nuts
250 g (9 oz) unsalted butter, softened
220 g (7¾ oz/1 cup) caster (superfine) sugar
200 ml (7 fl oz) fresh orange juice
2 tablespoons finely grated orange zest
300 g (10½ oz/2 cups) self-raising flour
4 large free-range eggs, beaten

CREAM CHEESE ICING (FROSTING)
250 g (9 oz) cream cheese, softened
50 g (1¾ oz) unsalted butter, softened
1 tablespoon finely grated orange zest
185 g (6½ oz/1½ cups) pure icing (confectioners') sugar, sifted

---

Preheat the oven to 190°C (375°F). Lightly grease a 20 cm (8 inch) square cake tin and line the base and sides with baking paper.

Put the pistachio nuts in a small food processor and whiz to a fine crumb. Using an electric mixer, beat the butter and sugar together until pale and fluffy. Add the orange juice, orange zest and flour, then add the beaten egg, a little at a time, and stir until combined. Reserve 2 tablespoons of the ground pistachios for decorating, then fold the remaining pistachio nuts into the batter.

Spoon the batter into the prepared tin and bake for 50 minutes, or until a skewer inserted into the centre of the cake comes out clean. Remove from the oven and leave to cool in the tin.

To make the cream cheese icing, beat the cream cheese, butter and orange zest until smooth. Gradually add the icing sugar and beat until well incorporated.

Remove the cooled cake from the tin and transfer to a serving plate. Spread the icing over the top and sprinkle with the reserved pistachios.

SERVES 8–10

Chocolate, cranberry and coconut slice

When my brothers and I were children, we each had our favourite chocolate bar. I loved the chewy coconut centres of the Bounty bar and my eldest brother loved Cherry Ripes. He moved to England years ago, but my mother still sends him care packages full of his favourite Australian sweets.

This slice is a bit of an ode to those family memories. It's really a big square of chewy coconut macaroon, sandwiched between thick dark chocolate and scattered with little bits of tart cranberry, but to me it's a happy reminder of rare childhood treats.

105 g (3¾ oz/²/3 cup) dried cranberries, roughly chopped
2 tablespoons boiling water
4 egg whites
150 g (5½ oz/²/3 cup) caster (superfine) sugar
225 g (8 oz/2½ cups) desiccated coconut
100 g (3½ oz) good-quality dark chocolate (70% cocoa), chopped

Preheat the oven to 150°C (300°F). Lightly grease a 20 cm (8 inch) square cake tin and line the base and sides with baking paper.

Put the cranberries in a bowl and cover with the boiling water. Leave the cranberries to soak until they have absorbed all the water. In a separate bowl, whisk the egg whites until frothy, then add the sugar and continue to whisk for 1 minute before adding the coconut and soaked cranberries.

Press the mixture evenly into the prepared tin and smooth the top. Bake for 30 minutes, or until the top is golden brown. Remove and set aside to cool.

Meanwhile, put the chopped chocolate in a small heatproof bowl over a saucepan of simmering water, ensuring the base of the bowl does not touch the water. Stir occasionally until the chocolate has melted, then remove the bowl from the heat.

Turn the coconut slice out onto a wire rack, top side down, and remove the baking paper. Spread two-thirds of the melted chocolate over the base and transfer to the refrigerator to chill and set. When set, turn the slice over and drizzle the remaining chocolate over the top (warm the chocolate if it has set). Allow the chocolate to set, then cut into squares.

MAKES 25 SQUARES

Energy bars

Full of oaty, fruity goodness, these energy bars are perfect for that mid-afternoon sugar slump. They are also great for lunchboxes, picnics or, dare I say it, a hasty breakfast.

160 g (5½ oz) coconut oil
175 g (6 oz/½ cup) honey
190 g (6¾ oz/2 cups) rolled (porridge) oats
100 g (3½ oz/1 cup) desiccated coconut
65 g (2¼ oz/⅓ cup) chia seeds
80 g (2¾ oz/½ cup) currants
180 g (6½ oz/1 cup) sliced pitted prunes
145 g (5 oz/1 cup) dried cranberries, chopped
3 large free-range eggs, beaten

Preheat the oven to 170°C (325°F). Lightly grease a 19 x 25 cm (7½ x 10 inch) cake tin and line the base and sides with baking paper.

Put the coconut oil and honey in a small saucepan over medium heat and stir until the oil has melted.

Combine the oats, coconut, chia seeds and dried fruit in a bowl, then add the warm honey mixture and eggs and stir to combine well. Press the mixture evenly into the prepared tin.

Bake for 30 minutes, or until the mixture is cooked through and the top is golden brown. Remove from the oven and cool in the tin before cutting into rectangular bars.

SERVES 12

Apple crumble cake

When it comes to cakes, I like mine gutsy and real. I can easily walk past a fine patisserie display of creamy layers, teetering chocolate or mille-feuille madness, but show me a cake bursting with summer fruits, ground nuts or trails of messy brown sugar and the concept of 'no' escapes me. This is one of those cakes that I will always fall victim to. Packed with spicy apples and topped with a sweet brown sugar crumble, it's a winner in my book.

CRUMBLE TOPPING
50 g (1³/₄ oz/¹/₂ cup) quick-cook rolled (porridge) oats
45 g (1¹/₂ oz/¹/₂ cup) desiccated coconut
60 g (2¹/₄ oz/¹/₄ cup, firmly packed) light brown sugar
50 g (1³/₄ oz) unsalted butter, melted

180 g (6¹/₂ oz) unsalted butter, softened
220 g (7³/₄ oz/1 cup) caster (superfine) sugar
4 large free-range eggs, separated
150 g (5¹/₂ oz/1 cup) plain (all-purpose) flour, sifted
1 teaspoon ground cinnamon
a generous pinch of ground cardamom
2 teaspoons baking powder
100 g (3¹/₂ oz/1 cup) almond meal
1 kg (2 lb 4 oz) green apples, such as granny smiths, peeled
    and coarsely chopped
icing (confectioners') sugar, for dusting

Preheat the oven to 170°C (325°F). Lightly grease a 24 cm (9¹/₂ inch) spring-form cake tin and line the base and side with baking paper.

To make the crumble topping, combine all the ingredients in a bowl and set aside.

Using an electric mixer, beat the butter and sugar together until light and fluffy, then add the egg yolks, one at a time, beating well after each addition. Continue to beat for a further 3 minutes, or until creamy. Fold in the sifted flour, cinnamon, cardamom and baking powder and then stir in the almond meal.

Using an electric mixer, whisk the egg whites in a clean, small bowl until they form stiff peaks. Gently fold the egg white into the cake batter in two batches. Fold the chopped apple through the batter. Spoon the batter into the prepared tin and smooth the surface. Sprinkle the crumble mixture over the top.

Cover the top of the cake with a piece of foil and bake for 40 minutes, then remove the foil and bake for a further 30 minutes, or until a skewer inserted into the centre of the cake comes out clean. Leave the cake in the tin for 15 minutes, then transfer to a serving plate to cool. Dust with icing sugar and serve with whipped cream or ice cream, if desired.

SERVES 12

Pecan and coffee tea cake

In my opinion, this is one of those perfect afternoon tea cakes—it's not too rich but has lots of lovely spicy pecan flavours rippled through the centre of the cake. Serve it in thick slices, still warm from the oven, or when it's a couple of days old, lightly buttered ... that's if it lasts that long.

PECAN TOPPING
30 g (1 oz/¼ cup) pecans
3 teaspoons ground cinnamon
55 g (2 oz/¼ cup) caster (superfine) sugar

2 tablespoons instant coffee
1 tablespoon boiling water
60 g (2¼ oz) unsalted butter, softened
150 g (5½ oz/⅔ cup) caster (superfine) sugar
1 large free-range egg
130 g (4½ oz/½ cup) Greek-style yoghurt
150 g (5½ oz/1 cup) self-raising flour, sifted
10 g (¼ oz) butter, extra, melted

Preheat the oven to 180°C (350°F). Lightly grease a 9 x 20 cm (3½ x 8 inch) loaf (bar) tin and line the base and sides with baking paper.

To make the pecan topping, put the pecans in a small food processor and process to a fine crumb. Transfer to a bowl and stir in the cinnamon and sugar. Set aside.

Put the instant coffee in a small bowl and pour in the boiling water. Stir until dissolved.

To make the cake batter, use an electric mixer to beat the butter, sugar and egg in a small bowl until light and fluffy. Stir in the coffee and yoghurt, then gently fold in the sifted flour.

Spread half of the batter into the prepared loaf tin and sprinkle three-quarters of the pecan mixture over the top. Dollop the remaining batter over the pecan mixture and carefully smooth the top as well as you can.

Bake for 40–45 minutes, or until a skewer inserted into the centre of the cake comes out clean. Leave the cake in the tin for 5 minutes before turning out, top side up, onto a wire rack. Brush the top with the melted butter, then sprinkle with the remaining pecan topping. Slice and serve warm with a little butter.

SERVES 8–10

Chocolate chip cookies

These cookies really need no introduction, except to say that it's probably a good idea to make a double batch. Keep the extra batch of rolled cookie dough in the freezer and whip it out when you suddenly and unexpectedly find your house overrun with hungry children or surprise visitors. Serve with a tall glass of icy milk or a short cup of espresso coffee.

100 g (3½ oz) unsalted butter
150 g (5½ oz/⅔ cup, firmly packed) light brown sugar
3 tablespoons caster (superfine) sugar
1 teaspoon vanilla bean paste
1 large free-range egg
260 g (9¼ oz/1¾ cups) self-raising flour
½ teaspoon sea salt
80 g (2¾ oz) dark chocolate, finely chopped

Using an electric mixer, cream the butter and sugars until light and fluffy, then add the vanilla bean paste and egg, beating once more to combine. Sift the flour and sea salt into the butter mixture and continue to mix until well combined. Add the chopped chocolate and, using a wooden spoon, work it into the cookie dough.

Place a piece of baking paper on the work surface and shape the dough into a line along the centre of the paper. Using your hands, roll the dough into a log that is about 6 cm (2½ inches) in diameter. Wrap the log in the paper and chill in the refrigerator for 1 hour.

Meanwhile, preheat the oven to 180°C (350°F). Line two baking trays with baking paper.

Cut the log into 1 cm (½ inch) thick slices and place on the prepared trays, spacing them 5–6 cm (2–2½ inches) apart to allow for spreading. Bake for 8–10 minutes, or until golden. Allow the cookies to cool on the trays for a few minutes before transferring to a wire rack.

MAKES 30

Peanut butter jam drops

As a child watching American TV shows, I never quite understood what a peanut butter and jelly sandwich was. I had visions of the wobbly raspberry jelly that Mum sometimes whipped up to go with our peaches and ice cream for dessert. Of course nowadays everyone loves their salted caramel and wouldn't blink at such a combination, but in the seventies salt never met sweet!

Then one day I was making peanut butter melting moments, and decided that they needed a bit of extra sweetness. Suddenly memories of Marcia, Jan and the whole Brady Bunch came rushing back to me, and these biscuits were born.

60 g (2¼ oz) smooth peanut butter
40 g (1½ oz) unsalted butter, softened
55 g (2 oz/¼ cup, firmly packed) light brown sugar
1 large free-range egg
½ teaspoon sea salt
75 g (2½ oz/½ cup) plain (all-purpose) flour
45 g (1½ oz/¼ cup) rice flour
80 g (2¾ oz/¼ cup) strawberry jam
icing (confectioners') sugar, for dusting

Preheat the oven to 160°C (315°F). Line two baking trays with baking paper.

Using an electric mixer, cream the peanut butter, butter and brown sugar and then add the egg. Beat for a further 1 minute, then fold in the sea salt, plain flour and rice flour. Cover and refrigerate for 30 minutes.

Roll heaped teaspoons of the mixture into small balls and place on the baking trays, spacing them about 5 cm (2 inches) apart to allow for spreading. Lightly press your thumb into the centre of each ball and drop ¼ teaspoon of jam into the hollows.

Bake for about 15 minutes, or until the biscuits are golden brown. Remove and transfer to a wire rack to cool. Dust with icing sugar before serving or storing in an airtight container.

MAKES 25

Nectarine and rosewater cake

It's the floral perfume of the rosewater that makes this cake come alive in a beautifully light, summery way. I've used nectarines because of their soft skins, but you could also use soft berries or peaches that have been poached or have had their skins removed.

I like to use raw caster sugar in this cake, because it gives a subtle caramel tone to the base mixture; however, if you have trouble finding it, then white caster sugar can be used instead.

110 g (3³/₄ oz/¹/₂ cup, firmly packed) light brown sugar
60 ml (2 fl oz/¹/₄ cup) white wine
1 teaspoon vanilla bean paste
500 g (1 lb 2 oz) ripe nectarines
330 g (11¹/₂ oz/1¹/₂ cups) raw (or golden) caster (superfine) sugar
185 ml (6 fl oz/³/₄ cup) vegetable oil
3 large free-range eggs
2 teaspoons rosewater
260 g (9¹/₄ oz/1 cup) Greek style yoghurt
375 g (13 oz/2¹/₂ cups) self-raising flour, sifted

Preheat the oven to 180°C (350°F). Lightly grease a 24 cm (9¹/₂ inch) round cake tin and line the base and side with baking paper.

Put the brown sugar, wine and vanilla bean paste in a small saucepan. Cook over medium heat for about 5 minutes, or until the sugar has dissolved and has become a thick syrup. Remove from the heat and pour the syrup into the base of the prepared tin.

Slice the nectarines into 5 mm (¹/₄ inch) thick slices and arrange them over the base of the cake tin, starting in the centre of the tin and working outwards in a fanning flower pattern.

Using an electric mixer, beat the caster sugar, oil, eggs and rosewater until well combined. Add the yoghurt and beat until the batter is smooth, then fold in the sifted flour. Carefully pour the batter into the tin over the nectarines and smooth the top.

Bake for 40 minutes, or until a skewer inserted into the centre of the cake comes out clean. Leave the cake in the tin to cool, then turn out onto a serving plate. Serve with whipped cream or custard.

SERVES 10

Green apple tart

This tart is all about the pure flavour of the apples, but it does need a good base so either make your own pastry or invest in a good-quality butter pastry.

I always grate the entire apple, including the skin, because it gives a lovely colour and texture to the tart, so it's worth buying organic and unwaxed apples. If organic apples aren't available, then give your apples a thorough wash under warm water or peel them before grating.

1 sheet frozen butter shortcrust pastry, thawed
60 g (2¼ oz) unsalted butter
60 g (2¼ oz/¼ cup) caster (superfine) sugar
2 organic green apples, such as granny smiths
1 teaspoon vanilla bean paste
1 teaspoon lemon juice
2 large free-range eggs, beaten
icing (confectioners') sugar, for dusting

Preheat the oven to 200°C (400°F). Generously grease an 18 x 27 cm (7 x 10¾ inch) rectangular tart (flan) tin with a removable base.

Press the pastry sheet into the tin. Trim the edges and then chill in the refrigerator for 30 minutes.

Line the pastry case with crumpled baking paper and fill with baking beads, uncooked rice or dried beans. Put the tin on a baking tray and bake for 15 minutes, then remove the weights and return to the oven for a further 5 minutes, or until the pastry looks dry and golden brown. Remove the tart case from the oven and reduce the oven temperature to 180°C (350°F).

Put the butter in a small saucepan over medium heat and cook until the butter begins to bubble and turn a dark nutty brown. Remove from the heat and transfer to a bowl. Add the sugar and stir to dissolve. Coarsely grate the apples and add them to the butter mixture. Add the vanilla bean paste and lemon juice and stir well to combine. Add the beaten egg and stir to combine.

Spoon the apple mixture into the tart case and bake for 15–20 minutes, or until the apples are soft and cooked through. Serve with a dusting of icing sugar.

SERVES 8

Orange passion biscuits

These are a beautiful Italian-style biscuit to which I've added a dash of zesty Australian flavour with the fresh passionfruit juice. They're crisp and tart, with an interesting texture from the semolina, and just perfect to nibble on with your favourite coffee.

60 g (2¼ oz) unsalted butter, melted
2 tablespoons extra virgin olive oil
1 tablespoon passionfruit juice
1 large free-range egg
2 tablespoons finely grated orange zest
110 g (3¾ oz/½ cup) caster (superfine) sugar
150 g (5½ oz/1 cup) plain (all-purpose) flour, sifted
95 g (3¼ oz/½ cup) coarse semolina
1 teaspoon baking powder
a good pinch of salt
icing (confectioners') sugar, for dusting

In a bowl, whisk together the melted butter, olive oil, passionfruit juice and egg. Stir in the orange zest, sugar, sifted flour, semolina, baking powder and salt. Turn the dough out onto a long piece of baking paper and shape it into a long roll about 4 cm (1½ inches) in diameter. Wrap the dough in the paper and chill in the refrigerator for 30 minutes.

Meanwhile, preheat the oven to 180°C (350°F). Line two baking trays with baking paper.

Slice the dough into 1 cm (½ inch) thick discs and place on the prepared trays, spacing them about 3 cm (1¼ inches) apart to allow for spreading. Bake the biscuits for 12 minutes, or until golden brown.

Leave the biscuits on the trays for 5 minutes before transferring to a wire rack to cool. Dust with icing sugar and store in an airtight container.

MAKES 40

Chocolate cake

I call this cake the Goldilocks chocolate cake because it's not too heavy and not too light and so sits somewhere in the middle, at just about right!

As such, it's more of an afternoon tea cake than a dessert cake, though feel free to decorate it with chocolate shards or nutty praline if you'd like a more showy affair. You can make a traditional chocolate ganache to use as an icing or combine some of the leftovers from the tub of sour cream with melted chocolate, but I like the texture of this coconut milk version.

100 g (3½ oz) dark chocolate, chopped
125 g (4½ oz) unsalted butter, softened
110 g (3¾ oz/½ cup, firmly packed) light brown sugar
1 teaspoon natural vanilla extract
3 large free-range eggs
60 ml (2 fl oz/¼ cup) maple syrup
100 g (3½ oz) sour cream
2 tablespoons unsweetened cocoa powder, sifted
75 g (2½ oz/½ cup) self-raising flour, sifted
a pinch of sea salt
150 g (5½ oz/1½ cups) almond meal

CHOCOLATE ICING (FROSTING)
100 g (3½ oz) dark chocolate, chopped and melted
80 ml (2½ fl oz/⅓ cup) coconut milk

Preheat the oven to 170°C (325°F). Lightly grease a 20 cm (8 inch) square cake tin and line the base and sides with baking paper.

Put the chopped chocolate in a small heatproof bowl over a saucepan of simmering water, ensuring the base of the bowl does not touch the water. Stir occasionally until the chocolate has melted, then remove the bowl from the heat.

Using an electric mixer, beat the butter, brown sugar and vanilla until pale and creamy. Add the eggs, one at a time, beating well after each addition. Add the maple syrup, sour cream and melted chocolate and beat until just combined. Fold in the sifted cocoa, flour and sea salt, then the almond meal.

Spoon the batter into the prepared tin and smooth the surface. Bake for 40–50 minutes, or until a skewer inserted into the centre of the cake comes out clean. Cool in the tin for 10 minutes before turning out onto a wire rack. Cool completely before icing.

To make the chocolate icing, combine the melted chocolate in a bowl with the coconut milk. Set aside for 10 minutes to cool and thicken a little, then spread the icing over the cooled cake.

SERVES 8–10

White chocolate and strawberry sponge

An old-fashioned favourite with a little white chocolate twist, this is the perfect cake to share with a gossipy bunch of girlfriends. It should be served on your prettiest plate with your favourite mixed set of teacups and cake plates, next to a vase filled with country cottage flowers, fresh from the garden.

80 g (2¾ oz) white chocolate, chopped
125 g (4½ oz) unsalted butter, chopped
4 large free-range egg whites
165 g (5¾ oz/¾ cup) caster (superfine) sugar
2 large free-range egg yolks
75 g (2½ oz/½ cup) plain (all-purpose) flour, sifted
3 tablespoons strawberry jam, warmed
300 ml (10½ fl oz) cream, whipped
250 g (9 oz/1 punnet) strawberries, hulled and halved

Preheat the oven to 180°C (350°F). Lightly grease a 20 cm (8 inch) round cake tin and line the base and side with baking paper.

Put the chocolate and butter in a small heatproof bowl over a saucepan of simmering water, ensuring the base of the bowl does not touch the water. Stir occasionally until the chocolate and butter have melted, then remove the bowl from the heat.

Using an electric mixer with the whisk attachment, whisk the egg whites until soft peaks form. While still beating, slowly add the sugar and continue to whisk until the egg whites are firm and glossy.

Transfer the warm chocolate mixture to a large bowl and, using a hand-held whisk, whisk in the two egg yolks, one at a time. When they are well combined, gently fold the sifted flour through the mixture. Spoon half of the egg white into the chocolate mixture and gently stir to combine, then fold in the remaining egg white.

Spoon the batter into the prepared tin and bake for 20 minutes, or until firm. Leave the cake to cool in the tin, then turn out onto a serving plate. This cake will dip a little in the middle as it cools, but that's fine as it provides a perfect nest for the whipped cream and strawberries.

When ready to serve, spread the jam over the top of the cake, then add the whipped cream. Top with the strawberries and serve.

SERVES 8–10

Index

Acknowledgements

If someone had asked me, as a young girl, what I wanted to do when I grew up, the answer would always have been 'book illustrator'. So, how wonderful it is that I've finally been given the chance to draw over one of my books!

This book has been very much a personal project and I've been fortunate through the process to work with many of my favourite people. My heartfelt thanks must therefore go to Sue Hines and Corinne Roberts for firstly giving me the chance to do this book, and secondly giving me the freedom to see my vision through to the end. Indeed, thank you to the whole team at Murdoch Books for providing such an encouraging and supportive environment. Thank you to Emma Hutchinson, who maintained the momentum of the book and ensured that we all stayed on track. Kim Rowney passed a critical editorial eye over my recipes, asked lots of necessary questions and waved a magical wand over my words — thank you for all you did to bring the book together. Speaking of words, they must have a place and their own visual weight and for this I must thank the joyous Vivien Valk for her beautiful design. Viv took my original concept, gave it a bit of a polish and then worked tirelessly to keep the crisp freshness of the book alive. Thank you so much for all your hard work and, yet again, it has been an absolute pleasure to create a book with you.

Speaking of creativity, I had the dream team in the studio. Kirsten Jenkins generously shared her extraordinary talents in the kitchen, bringing my recipes to life. She arrived each morning with a big smile, boxes of perfect produce and boundless energy. Thank you for all the hard work, laughter and beautiful food.

Petrina Tinslay and I have worked together for 15 years through various books, magazines and projects and I never tire of seeing the magic she brings to each image. Thank you so much for the beautiful lighting, extraordinary eye for detail and the calm Zen that you bring not only to the photos but also the studio. And not to mention the odd glasses of champagne we've shared through the years!

Away from the book, normal life must go on and I must thank the following people for all their support throughout this project. A very big thank you to Fran Abdallaoui, who has been not only a generous colleague but also a great friend. Thank you also to all the playground mums who provide daily inspiration and friendship, and lastly a heartfelt thank you to my parents who raised me with an 'I can' attitude.

As Virginia Woolf once wrote, a room of one's own is essential to any creative process, and for giving me the space to write I must extend a huge thank you to the two men in my life, Sam and Si. Sometimes that room can just be a peaceful home, a calm kitchen and spare quiet moments to think about food. Thank you for giving me the time to write and for allowing scrawled recipes, manuscripts, odd bowls of food, pens and paper to cover the kitchen table!

Published in 2015 by Murdoch Books,
an imprint of Allen & Unwin

Murdoch Books Australia
83 Alexander Street
Crows Nest NSW 2065
Phone: +61 (0)2 8425 0100
Fax: +61 (0)2 9906 2218
murdochbooks.com.au
info@murdochbooks.com.au

Murdoch Books UK
Erico House, 6th Floor
93–99 Upper Richmond Road
Putney, London SW15 2TG
Phone: +44 (0) 20 8785 5995
murdochbooks.co.uk
info@murdochbooks.co.uk

For Corporate Orders & Custom Publishing contact Noel Hammond,
National Business Development Manager, Murdoch Books Australia

Publisher: Corinne Roberts
Editorial Manager: Emma Hutchinson
Editor: Kim Rowney
Designer: Vivien Valk
Photographer: Petrina Tinslay
Illustrator and Stylist: Michele Cranston
Food Preparation: Kirsten Jenkins
Production Manager: Mary Bjelobrk

A cataloguing-in-publication entry is available from the catalogue
of the National Library of Australia at nla.gov.au.

ISBN 978 1 74336 539 7 Australia
ISBN 978 1 74336 555 7 UK

A catalogue record for this book is available from the British Library.

Colour reproduction by Splitting Image Colour Studio Pty Ltd,
Clayton, Victoria, Australia
Printed by 1010 Printing International Limited, China

IMPORTANT: Those who might be at risk from the effects of salmonella
poisoning (the elderly, pregnant women, young children and those suffering
from immune deficiency diseases) should consult their doctor with any
concerns about eating raw eggs.

OVEN GUIDE: You may find cooking times vary depending on the oven you
are using. For fan-forced ovens, as a general rule, set the oven temperature
to 20°C (35°F) lower than indicated in the recipe.

MEASURES GUIDE: We have used 20 ml (4 teaspoon) tablespoon measures.
If you are using a 15 ml (3 teaspoon) tablespoon add an extra teaspoon of
the ingredient for each tablespoon specified.